INSTABRAIN

THE NEW RULES FOR MARKETING TO GENERATION Z

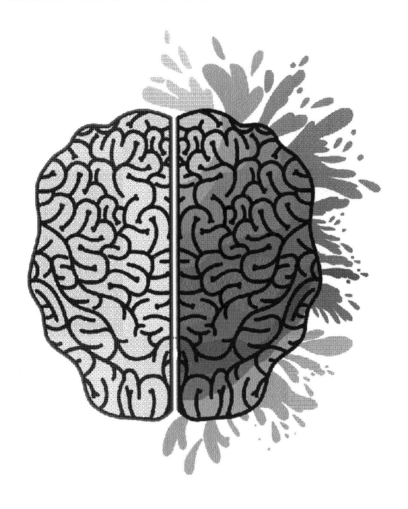

SARAH WEISE

ISBN-10: 1717836798
ISBN-13: 978-1717836793

Events in this book are based on the author's memories from the author's perspective. Portions of this book are works of nonfiction. Certain names and identifying characteristics have been changed.

Front cover by Sarah Weise.
Editing by Jon Wuebben.
Book design by Kevin Summers.

First printing edition 2019.

www.sarahweise.com

CONTENTS

"A game-changing approach to marketing, sales, and advertising. Sarah Weise writes in clear, jargon-free prose, and the stories and examples from both B2C and B2B were right on point. This new set of rules is the how-to guide your agency needs to create irresistible user experiences that engage and connect with this powerful generation of young consumers."

- **Michael Salamon,** Co-Founder of UX Masters Academy

"InstaBrain is instant insight.... Sarah Weise's research can take your marketing targeting to a whole new level. Stop assuming you know what Gen Z wants. Instead, read this book."

- **Ryan Foland,** 4-time TEDx speaker and Author of *Ditch the Act*

"Wow. I learned so much new information reading InstaBrain! Generation Z [bring] an honest, back-to-basics, can-do, work ethic ethos to all of us and have vastly different habits when they research and interact with a brand. Sarah Weise delivers this important information in a clear, comprehensive way. I couldn't put the book down! Highly recommended for ALL business people."

-**Jon Wuebben,** CEO, Content Launch and
Author, *Future Marketing: Winning in the Prosumer Age*

"Sarah Weise offers easy-to-apply strategies to help make you a better marketer in today's world. You will learn techniques that will change your strategy, whether you are marketing directly to youth or not. Amazing read and right on target."

- **Joni Rayos Samilin**, CEO, The Mindset Group

To Nick for your constant love and support.

I'd die of dysentery with you any day.

#OregonTrailGeneration

To Linna and Brianne for your unwavering enthusiasm

and stunning curiosity about the world around you.

You are my why.

#GenerationAlpha

INTRODUCTION

At the time I launched my first youth research study, I had been conducting research for nearly 15 years. I had identified customer trends, created psychographic personas, and built strategy for over 100 brands. I had gotten to know audiences ranging from tax dodgers to PBS donors, and after doing so much research, not much surprised me anymore.

Yet an early video that rolled in from a young lady in her early 20s blew my mind.

The task seemed simple: participants were asked to record their phone screens and show us how they keep up with an interest or hobby. With graceful ease, Alexis[1] bounded between no less than 6 apps on her phone to plan a weekend girls trip to Nashville.

She used no search engines.

She toggled between screens so fast it was like watching a symphony conductor unify an orchestra in prestissimo. Within just 10 minutes, she had soaked in extensive research on her trip, and had planned nearly every aspect of it from flights to hotels to activities, even what outfit she would wear while at the zoo! She had found Groupons for activities and had scouted the best food and nightlife. She knew just what hashtags to "search up" and she analyzed photos on Instagram with intuitive precision: "This club looks slow. He snapped a photo after 11 and there's not even a line." Setting the tempo, she was then able to execute clear preparations, sharing itineraries through Airbnb with her travel companions.

All this, in just 10 minutes!

Yet in my mind, the most impressive part was that this was no big deal for Alexis.

For me, finding the ideal combination of departure times and airfare for any trip is a major headache. Alexis flew through this research step, processing times and dates and layovers and airport combinations with ease.

While zooming through pages, she shared her thoughts on brand loyalty, without anyone even asking: "So I am building a better relationship with Google Flights than I am with Skyscanner because I am seeing that… Google Flights has more information."

In that study alone, we collected over 30,000 data points across two countries, and paired quantitative research indicating scale with deep pscyhographic interviews and in-home ethnographic research. Basically, I spent six months hanging out with teenagers. The "fam" as it were.

After that, I did many more studies focusing on this intriguing generation. Needless to say, I had a lot of stories to choose from when authoring this work. But I picked Alexis' story to share here because she is the quintessential representation of Generation Z. From this initial interaction, we as marketers could learn an unbelievable amount about attention, retention, brand awareness, searching, inspiration, researching, converting, transacting, sharing, and so much more!

It is March 2019 at the time of this publication, and in just a few short months, Generation Z will assume the position as the largest generation in the United States, representing 40 percent of American consumers![2] Consider that for a moment—this relatively unknown generation (by marketing standards) is about to overtake nearly half of consumers out there. If that is not enough to convince your company to shift your marketing research focus from Millennials to this younger, more influential generation, well, read on. But sit down, because these stats might just make you dizzy.

This group of teens and young 20-somethings represent $44 billion in *direct* buying power[3]. Just imagine how that number will surge once they get jobs after college!

When you include what parents and caregivers spend on Generation Z today, this purchase power skyrockets to $255 billion. Additionally, when you add in total household expenditures, the impact of Generation Z's influence on other household spending may be more than $655 billion.[4]

Moreover, this generation is wielding their mighty influence on every other generation, in just about every industry. And yet, the marketing departments of many organizations are still focusing on Millennial research and are missing the gigantic potential of Generation Z.

With this book, I hope to inspire you to shift your focus in a very strategic way. The time to start your research is now. This large and financially-responsible group wields never-before-seen influence on our consumer markets. However, marketing to this group will not be a walk in the park. This generation has high standards for themselves and even higher standards for the brands around them to live up to. Brand loyalty with this group is harder to achieve than with any other generation.

So let's get to work!

In *InstaBrain*, I will:

- Prove to you why marketing to Generation Z is worth your time, even if they are not your direct target audience

- Show you that your past research no longer applies; this generation demands a different approach

- Walk you through key trends about this generation that will matter to you, and provide marketing takeaways within each section

- Offer a set of *new* rules for marketing and brand-building to this critical consumer group

In sharing these trends and tactics with you, it is my hope that you walk away with an actionable plan to not just survive but thrive with this new wave of customers, the influential and mighty Generation Z.

Sarah Weise

hello@sarahweise.com

www.sarahweise.com

PART I: THE CHALLENGE

"I love, love, *love* James Charles."

These were the first words 13-year-old Kira declared as I started to set up for an interview with her. I was there to talk about beauty, and how she engages with this topic on her phone. Over the next few weeks as I continued these interviews, I would hear these same lyrics echoed over and over, reverberating through bedrooms and bouncing off kitchen tables of teens across the country.

I have to admit that before getting to know hundreds of teens and young adults, I did not have the slightest idea who James Charles was. I now know James Charles to be *the* beauty icon of this generation. If you do not know who this is, get to your phone—stat—and then thank the good Lord that you picked up this book, because your business strategy (and possibly your eyebrows) are about to change.

....

I often speak at conferences, but my favorite part is not actually the speaking. It is that quiet moment before the conference starts, when you arrive early to do an audio check. The seats are empty, but the hum of the floodlights and the warmth emanating from the audio equipment shoots a buzz of excitement into the air. This is the *best* part because of the energy, the promise. In just a short amount of time, I know that the seats will be packed with people who are about to learn the secrets of marketing to Generation Z. I also know that once they learn it, they will never be able to look at a teen in exactly the same way. And once they start applying it, their business will never be the same.

Many companies are still caught up in the Millennial whirlwind, and they overlook Generation Z. They have no awareness that the next consumer powerhouse is not just coming—it has arrived.

YOUR PAST RESEARCH NO LONGER APPLIES

What is the biggest mistake people make in a crisis? Not knowing when they're in a crisis.

- Olivia Pope, Scandal

What you know about your customers right now, at this moment, is not enough to keep your business or your product alive. Why? Because your past customer research is no longer valid.

Consider for a moment how much you invest in your customer personas. As the astute marketer that you are, you likely follow best practices and construct personas or profiles for each of your products and services—illustrative representations of your target audiences, grounded in customer research.

Based on these personas, you develop marketing strategies, craft content and pay for advertising based on the assumptions within. When you are basing your company's future success on these types of personas, they *better* be right.

Whether or not you are marketing directly to the youth segment, they are without a doubt changing the game. Never before has a generation's behavior and mindset rippled up through other generations and affected all other demographics. Generation Z is having a big impact on your business today, even if you don't realize it yet.

Need proof? Ask yourself this: when was the last time you texted an emoji or took a selfie? Was it 5 minutes ago? Or 10 minutes ago? Today's teens and young adults are influencing just about every other audience to do things differently.

Take my mother, for example. At almost 70 years old, I never thought she would own a smart phone—much less be FaceTiming my kids every night at dinnertime. A few weeks ago, I was visiting for dinner, and my mother was sitting on the couch. We were chatting and she was distracted by her phone. She was clearly scanning some sort of feed, moving her finger up with habitual precision.

"Are you on Facebook," I asked, bewildered?

"Oh God, no," she replied, "That's not secure at all, fake news and data breaches... I'm on the Weight Watchers app."

I stared, perplexed, but intrigued.

"It's my online tribe," she shrugged in explanation.

So... I want to pause right there. My mother, someone who I've actually heard mutter the sentence, "I'll just pull up The Google on the FoxFire," used the term "online tribe" to describe a community feed she follows. Woah.

Your future customers have never known a world without search, social, and smart phones—and they are not just influencing future products; they are changing the game for just about every generation and every industry *today*.

B2B readers: pay attention now. This generation will influence your marketing strategy as well. They will be your buyers and your sellers and your partners. You must understand this generation in order to keep doing business in the future. Their mindsets, thought processes, and negotiation strategies are incredibly different than what you might expect based on your research of young Millennials just a few years older.

Consider this statistic: 51 percent of the world's population is under the age of 25.[5] Over half! And if the stereotype is true: wow, that is a lot of brunch.

More than that, 98 percent of teens in the world own a smart-phone (this is slightly lower in the U.S., around 96 percent).[6] Yes, I know… How many more selfies at brunch can we add to the world?? My goodness, that is a game changer. This is a generation that truly prefers their phone to their laptop (except in a few rare cases—like when they're doing homework).

What's more, 85 percent find out about new products through social media. You have probably come across a stat like this before, but the interesting thing here is that most of their discovery is through people: friends and family and influencers, not typically through the sponsored ads that your company has likely been paying for.

In fact, we no longer have merely influencers, those "Internet-famous" few with millions of followers. We now have microinfluencers—those with social media audiences ranging from tens of thousands to hundreds of thousands—and even nanoinflu-encers.[7] With as few as 1,000 followers, nanoinfluencers are some of the most sought-after by astute markers today. The New York Times says, "Their lack of fame is one of the qualities that make them approachable." Not only are they easy to deal with and seen as more authentic by their followers, they will pretty much will say anything companies ask them to, in exchange for a small commission. It's a win-win.

Your company may be investing heavily in millennial research. But if you are looking more than a year ahead in your strategic plan (as in, you want your brand to survive long-term), you are at a critical crossroad that demands a shift in focus.

You might be thinking, "How different could these generations be, really? These kids are just a few years apart."

Ok, I'll play. Let's list out all the similarities between Millennials and Generation Z.

Here is your rundown: these two generations, only a few years apart, both embrace technology, and have become accustomed to on-demand services from transportation to food delivery to streaming television. They share an addiction to social media and the sleep deprivation that goes with it. They have few close friends but gratuitous networks of "friends." They both have instant visibility into the lives of others, acquaintances and influencers alike, and they expect active engagement and co-creation with brands.[8] They both want to do good in the world.

And that is where the similarities end. That's right, just one paragraph! So glad I wrote a book on *that*.

The point here is simple: Generation Z is radically different than Millennials, and marketers require new, fresh research in order to connect with them, build relationships, and ultimately, count them as customers.

TODAY WE ARE DESIGNING EXPERIENCES FOR TOMORROW'S CUSTOMERS

Fact: Your current actions create your future. We know that this group of teens and young adults views the world and your brand experiences differently than other generations. We also know that this group is changing the way all other generations are interacting with technology, with brands, and even with each other. So remind me again: why aren't you already studying them? Marketers seem to be obsessed with Millennial research, but there is a new kid in town and we need to shift focus.

If you want to know what the future holds for your company or product, look to your actions today. Are you actively planning for the future? You picked up this book, so that's a good sign that you are thinking ahead beyond today's buyers, customers, partners, employees.

Just as you can predict your future health based on your eating and exercise habits today, so too can a company, brand, organization, product, service or anything else for that matter.

Today we are designing experiences for tomorrow's customers. The world is changing. Our future customers are so different than our current customers that we have to design different experiences for them. Whether you're B2C or B2B, you are affected because there is a brand new wave of people buying all kinds of products and services. We need to figure out how they operate because it is very different than it was even five years ago.

If you want to know how your business will need to adapt in the future, your research should start now. Today.

If you need any more convincing, just look to the graveyard of brand relics: think Toys R Us, Blockbuster, Borders Books & Music, Kodak, Palm Pilot, Google Plus, and so many more. These brands are extinct for a reason: they were replaced by a new way of doing business due to a new wave of customer expectations.

This necropolis of brands and products failed to pay attention to the coming tide of customer needs and expectations. What if the product owners and executive decision-makers had taken another direction instead? Would things have turned out differently? We will never know. What we do know is that these particular brands did not pay attention to the trends and needs of future customers, and how those future customers were impacting the expectations of existing customers. As a result… well, you know the rest.

Companies who don't bother to understand how future customers think, find information, transact, and communicate (or, worse yet, those who believe it does not apply to them) wind up as relics, as stories we tell in pithy marketing books and in keynote speeches at business conferences.

The reality: Your actions today—how well you are getting to know your future customers—could mean the difference between future success or failure.

For help creating your research strategy, visit www.sarahweise. com/training or email hello@sarahweise.com.

Z VS. MILLENNIAL: THE GENERATIONAL DIFFERENCES

Generational changes make for vastly different patterns in behavior and content consumption. While both Millennials and Generation Z are digital natives in the sense that they have grown up in a world of instant communication, they do not consume the same types of content. In contrast to Millennials, Generation Z was raised in an environment of economic instability and social change, churning out a generation of strong, resolute, earnest, hard working, entrepreneurial, responsible teens and young adults. As I write this, it feels strange and awkward to string "responsible" and "teens" together in a sentence, but for this generational cohort, it is true.

What are the generational traits that drive the way these two very different generations experience and interact in the world? We will cover it completely, from every angle. But first, a slight detour…

How Old Are They, Exactly?

Ah, it is finally here. The point at which someone inevitably asks me to name the extremely specific age range of a Millennial versus a member of Generation Z.

"Well, if I'm 35 and three-quarters, am I technically considered a Millennial?"

If you really raised your hand in a Q&A at a conference in front of a room full of people and asked me that question… Yes. Yes, you are.

KIDDING!

While no one can quite agree on the age ranges, these birth years should give you a general sense of where today's modern-day generations fall. I expect there might be 1-2 generations mentioned here that you might not recognize right away, and that's ok. Just read on...

The Silent Generation: 1928-1945

Baby Boomers: 1946-1964

Generation X: 1965-1981

Oregon Trail Generation: 1979-1982 (micro-generation)

Generation Y / Millennials: 1983-1994

Generation Z: 1995-2006

Generation Alpha: 2007 or later

Looking at this list, you might notice that these generations are "fluid". The reason that no one can quite agree on the start and end years is that generations are defined by more than just when you were born. Everything we see growing up—family, technology, communication, food, music, movies, fashion, transportation—shapes a shared cultural DNA between people who grew up experiencing the same things. For instance, let's say you were born in the late 70s or early 80s. You had big hair, were addicted to MTV, and you know what "sike" means. You are a millennial, right? Well, maybe. But then again, maybe not.

If you are in this age range and wondering what cohort you fall into, here is a more telling question:

Did you have high-speed Internet in your home while you were in high school?

I mean, real high-speed Internet. Not dial-up. Forget the AOL CDs. Yes, there were a lot, probably because the technology wasn't there to push an update directly. And no, they will never be collector's items—throw them away, you hoarder (you know who you are).

If you had high-speed Internet in your home growing up, and you are between the ages of 25 and 35, you are probably a Millennial. But let's say you are 35 and you did not have high-speed Internet until you went to college. Maybe you lived in a rural area, maybe your family was on a budget, maybe your parents thought the Internet was a fad (ahem, mom and dad, I hope you're reading this). But you may not be Generation X either. Why do we always try to make things so black and white?

Based on my large-scale research of hundreds of people in their teens, twenties, thirties, and forties, I agree with some past researchers who have noticed a strange gap between about 35 and 42 years old: half-analog, half digital natives. These are the people who remember TV with bunny-ear antenna and probably spent a large portion of their 20s downloading illegal music on Napster. This micro-generation has been labeled the "Generation Catalano," the "Xennials," and even "The Lucky Ones" (yes, really). But in 2015, a name came about that I actually love…

The "Oregon Trail" generation.

As a proud member of this micro-generation, I take pride in being a part of the group that remembers playing the famous Oregon Trail computer game on a floppy disk—not the small floppy, the *big* floppy. If you are in this generation, in your grade school computer class you probably shared one computer with two other kids and you cheered each other on as you pioneered your trail, ate squirrel meat, and eventually died of dysentery. These late 70s and early 80s babies bridge the gap between X and Y with, "a healthy portion of Gen X grunge cynicism, and a dash of the unbridled optimism of Millennials."[9] What's more, this micro-generation was on the cusp of changes that essentially transformed modern life.

In my experience, true Millennials can be identified with two simple behavioral-based questions. You already know the first one: Did you have high-speed Internet at home in high school? The second one might surprise (and humor) you: Are you still on your parents' cell phone plan?

You might think I'm joking here, but I assure you I'm not. In our recruiting screeners for market research studies, these two questions have proven time and again to be reliable in understanding if someone in their mid-30s identifies more with Millennials, or if they behaviorally skew older.

The takeaway here is that a "generation" is not just a number. It is a group of people within the population who have shared experiences and a collective sense of history that influences how they think and act today.

I'm sure you can go to Google, type in "In what years were Millennials born" and find an answer box with a specific range (Ah, Google, you understand my need for quick information so well. If only Instant Pot cooking times could be displayed that easily!) But it is these kind of seemingly inflexible ranges that would cause an impassioned article titled, "F*** You, I'm Not A Millennial" to go viral on Medium.[10]

At this point, you might be asking who comes next? Who is younger than Generation Z, if this group of kids starts around age 13? With the alphabet ending, what do we call them? To be perfectly honest, I was hoping it would be like an Excel spreadsheet and go to

Generation AA. But I suppose once they got to double-D, somebody would have a sticky naming convention on their hands! The powers to be who name generations apparently switched alphabets on us and went Greek. So the kiddos today—the little ones who think they can turn on Netflix by swiping their hand across that large black monitor you call a TV—they are Generation Alpha.

When my daughter (born in 2011) was about 5, she asked me for a phone. I retorted, "Who would you call?" A bewildered look crossed her face as she repeated the question, "Call?" Now that's Generation Alpha!

So what is the lesson here? As marketers, we have a duty to learn the tenets of our consumer base, and deeply understand what makes our target audiences tick. To do that, we need to know the overarching differences between these generational groups to be able to draw conclusions about who we are marketing to. Our focus should always be consumer behavior over demographics alone.

The Early Years

When conducting research, one of the first trends that inevitably emerges from the data is how remarkably different Generation Z and Millennials seem to be in terms of attitudes, outlooks, expectations, and (ahem... conversion) behaviors. They are very different groups, and in large part, this is (not surprisingly) a product of how they were raised.

This is actually one of the reasons that Generation Z has been dubbed the "Pivotals"—because they have pivoted away from common Millennial behaviors (sprinted in the opposite direction, more like). Goodbye spiritual optimists who backpack through Europe, have quarter-life crises, and life coaches to tell them to live their true selves; Generation Z is the new kid in town, socially liberal but financially conservative, risk averse, honest with themselves and others, and altogether reminiscent of the hard-working, no-nonsense consumers from generations past. Like most findings, though, the "what" is easy; the "why" takes a little more digging into.

While both Millennials and members of Generation Z are digital natives, they do not consume the same types of content. These generational shifts are important for brands to understand so that they can tailor their content to appeal to behaviorally-segmented target audiences.

In just 10 years, monumental changes occurred, ranging from technology to parenting tactics to unemployment to politics and more. While there many possible traits have determined the way these two generations experience and interact in the world, here are a few of the shifts that I find most compelling, and worth sharing with fellow marketers like you:

- Parenting habits that have resulted in more independent, cautious youth

- A "recession" mindset that has led to a generation of entrepreneurial doers, conservative with money, and big on education and career advancement

- Increasing diversity that has bred liberal views on fairness and inclusion

- Endless visual stimulation which has increased multitasking, shortened attention spans, and even altered the brain to enable faster processing of visual inputs

It is mind-boggling to see how the differences between the ways in which these two generations think, act, and transact online can vary so substantially, especially since many of them grew up in households with Millennial siblings.

Parenting Shift Resulting In More Independence And Resilience

Let's just put it out there: Millennials tend to get a bad rap. Other generations look down on this group, tossing up memes of everything from their need for positive affirmation to their love of avocado toast.

Just for kicks, here are a handful of Millennial "Merit Badges" created by the esteemed website EatLiver.com:[11]

Speaking of kicks, for the Millennials reading this: for $130, you too can wear avocado toast on your feet. Saucony has you covered with sneakers inspired by your love affair with this trendy dish:[12]

Why do these types of funnies ring true? Millennial behavior is often viewed by other generations as naive and entitled. But Millennial behavior is largely a product of how they were raised, and the fact is that there has been a profound shift in parenting styles between parents of these two generations.

Parents of Millennials are often defined by the term "helicopter" or "tiger" parenting. These hovering parents churned out a generation of kids tethered to their moms and dads. We have talked about how most Millennials in their 30s, even if they are married, are still on their parents' cell phone plans (a fact that mystifies Generation X). But beyond the financial ties, as adults, Millennials tend to have a harder time making decisions on their own. One study participant told me that he has called his mother to ask her what type of milk he should buy in the grocery store. He was 30 years old.

Just a few short years later, as smart phones and social media spread through older generations, a shift in parenting occurred from "helicopter" parenting to "technology" parenting. Instead of finding information, making phone calls and doing things for their children, technology parents taught their children how to find information for themselves online. They armed them with the tools to do things on their own, teaching them about search engines, social media, and the risks involved with having an online presence.

As these technology parents began to prepare their children to rely on their own, they also did another really interesting thing with their children: they taught them all about the risks associated with going online. Today, these kids can spout off by route memory all the reasons why they should keep personal information private, ensure privacy settings are turned on and location services are turned off when using social media, and only share information with specific people. They also prefer not to leave a permanent record of everything they ever said online (Hello, Snapchat). These youth talk a lot about their career aspirations, and they are fully aware that employers are looking at their online profiles before delivering that offer. Some would say these parents used caution. I say they scared their kids shitless!

Educators have also contributed to suspicion online. Ask any high schooler in the U.S. today about their thoughts on Wikipedia and they will warn you never to use it. When you ask them where they go to find information for homework, oftentimes their first response is, "Well, I don't use Wikipedia!" They have been brainwashed by teachers to be skeptical of this source because anyone can contribute to it.

This generation is not only more cautious than previous generations online; this is a theme that permeates into other aspects of their lives as well. Growing up in uncertain times breeds a generational cohort that craves security. As a result, Generation Z is far more risk-averse than Millennials. They tend to avoid risky behaviors like underage drinking, drugs, and smoking.[13] Wearing a seatbelt is not even a consideration.[14]

This parenting shift has led to a number of really interesting psychographic differences between these generations. First, the perception of authority has shifted. At one time, parents were considered the single source of truth; now this authority has turned to Google. This is resulting in a generation of more independent teens able to find answers to their questions instead of asking a parental authority figure. They carefully curate online personalities, and many have five or more accounts on Instagram to share different types of information with different audiences. This fact alone is very different than any other generation.

Relying less on their parents as a primary authority figure does open the relationship for a new type of relationship to emerge. Increasingly, we see teens and their parents unabashedly share common interests, frequently enjoying the same music, movies, and hobbies. Instead of being embarrassed about being seen with their parents, Generation Z does not seem to mind and many enjoy spending time with their folks. They communicate openly, share challenges at school or with friends, and rely on their parents' suggested advice to help them. A 2016 study of U.S. family relationships illustrated that parents (mothers especially) are seen as role models and even heroes by their children, especially in Hispanic and African American households.[15]

Generation Z is also more likely to live in multi-generational households. This has taught them to be sharers and have a greater affinity and respect for the elderly. In fact, Generation Z shares many of the same traditional values as their grandparents, an interesting cross-generational development.[16] This confirms the idea that teens do not mind accepting advice from older family members, and often ask for their opinions.

Speaking of family structure, this generation has grown up experiencing a wide array of family compositions, from single parents to unmarried parents living together to remarried families to adopted families to grandparents living with families to same sex families and so many more. In fact, in 2016 a researcher coded all family types in the U.S. and came back with 10,276 different types of family make-ups.[17] In the 1960s, 4 in 10 households represented the traditional nuclear family. By 2013 when Generation Z (ages 7-18 at the time) was still mostly living at home, this had decreased to fewer than 2 in 10.[18]

Of course, parenting styles are not the only reason for the large shift in beliefs, attitudes, and behaviors. Unlike Millennials who were raised in a boom, Generation Z has witnessed hardship. Born after 9/11, this generation grew up in times of war and recession and uncertainty. They have seen parents lose jobs or take pay cuts, budget for groceries, clip coupons, and struggle to climb out of credit card debt. As a result, we do not see members of Generation Z taking a year off after college to "find themselves" or at 25 years old declaring that they are going through a "quarter-life crisis" (both of which are frequent with Millennials).

A Hunger For Work

Generation Z is focused and hungry for work—even as teenagers. 61 percent of teens long to start their own business instead of working for someone else.[19] Many have business-centered Instagram accounts that are already working to build them a following for a possible future business. All in all, Generation Z has high regard for money-earners. This generation is particularly drawn to YouTubers and Instagram creators who are paid and sponsored and making money for themselves online.

Generation Z is far more focused on making money than Millennials (some might say obsessed). When my team is recruiting participants to join youth studies, Generation Z recruits often try to negotiate a higher payment for their participation or ask for referral bonuses for having a friend join the study. While I often get asked this by participants who are members of Generation Z, not once have I received a similar question from a Millennial. Millennials are happy to participate in studies and take what is offered, but they do not attempt negotiation.

Expectations Around Diversity And Inclusion

Another key difference stems from Generation Z being raised in a time of unprecedented cultural diversity. Today's youth have never known the world without a black president, female presidential candidates, and legalized gay marriage in most states. As mentioned previously, they grew up amidst over 10,000 different types of family structures in the U.S.[20] On top of this, multiracial children are one of the fastest growing segments of the United States. In fact, the last three decades have seen a 400 percent increase in multiracial marriages in the U.S., with a 1,000 percent increase in Asian-white marriages.[21] In 2013, 10 percent of births were multiracial; in 1970, this number was only 1 percent.[22]

According to a 2019 Pew Research study, roughly one-third of Gen Zers know someone who uses gender-neutral pronouns. Nearly 6 in 10 Generation Z youth believe that online profiles or surveys that ask about a person's gender should include options other than "male" and "female", while only 5 in 10 Millennials and 4 in 10 who are older share this sentiment. Pew Research analysts believe that these findings speak more to exposure than to viewpoint, as roughly equal shares of Generation Z and Millennials say society should be more accepting of people who do not identify as either a man or a woman.[23]

Given these stats, it makes perfect sense that this generation would epitomize liberal views on race, gender, identity, and sexuality. A 2019 Pew Research Center report highlighted Generation Z as the most racially and ethnically diverse generation we have seen in modern America.

Technologically empowered and socially driven, this generation has arrived at a crucial moment in history. As Fromm and Read write, "While Millennials dreamed of changing the world, Gen Z is wide awake and poised to actually make the moves."[24]

However, because diversity was always just there, around them as they grew up, they never witnessed the battle it took to fight for civil rights, gender equality, equal pay, and more. The battle is for the history books; this generation views diversity and inclusion as a default, a given. These topics are not seen as a constant struggle, but rather, simply an expectation. They tend to immediately dismiss viewpoints on these topics that are different from their own, without a moment's thought: of course the earth is round and all people should be equal. Thus, while they embody liberal beliefs on this topic, they do not yet see the battle they will need to engage in to move these beliefs into something more than just a trending hashtag.

In the same way that this generation embraces diversity of race and gender, they also seem to be evaluating new ideas with a more open perspective. In their world, new products and services pop up all the time. Kickstarter was a constant presence while they were growing up, and as a result this generation is evaluating new products and new choices with a different perspective. Because they believe that anyone can do it or make it, loyalty is tougher than ever for brands to earn.

Their political sensitivities have driven expectations of diversity on a more fundamental, basic, elemental level than we have seen in the past, and their viewpoints on fairness are leading the charge.

More Multitasking, Less Attention

Another core difference between Generation Z and Millenials (even those just a few years older) is how these groups each multitask and focus their attention. Generation Z is accustomed to a barrage of data flooding them from all angles, at every moment of their lives. They multitask without even thinking about it, processing more information at once than any other generation before them.

Oftentimes Generation Z is made fun of for their microscopic attention spans. But in reality, something *had* to change. The deluge of information has increased so much that studies have shown that their brains may have actually evolved and physically changed in order to process, parse, and harness more information—at faster speeds.[25] A modern step in one of those gorilla-neanderthal-human cartoons, Generation Z has adapted to process information quicker than its predecessors, with the ability to filter and make decisions about content in 8 seconds or less.[26]

When we talk about multitasking, it is important to note that there is evidence to suggest that multitasking is not actually a way to focus on multiple things at once: it is a quick flexing of attention between different contexts. When you are "multitasking" you are (more accurately) "multi-flexing" your attention. On average, Millennials juggle 3 screens at once, meaning they could be playing a video game, reading a Reddit thread, and snapping photos to friends on Snapchat. This means that in their short-term memory, they are able to hop between 3 different contexts with different information and keep it all straight. Typically, this Millennial group has a 12-second attention span.

Now, if you think that being able to hold information from 3 different contexts at once is incredible, keep on reading. Because those are the stats for *Millennials*.

Generation Z is a whole new ballgame. On average, this slightly younger group juggles 5 screens at once instead of 3. This is a shift that commands attention because it is a 67 percent increase! Between kids who are only a few years apart in age, it seems unimaginable that the numbers would be that different. That means that while Generation Z is playing a video game, commenting on a Reddit thread and keeping up their streak on Snapchat, they are also FaceTiming one group of friends, and texting another group of friends. I am not making this up: this group of teens is something straight out of a science fiction film. Generation X and Boomers get dizzy just thinking about it.

Of course, there are two sides to the coin. Because of this [misconception of multi-tasking] meteoric increase in attention flexing, the attention spans of this younger generation have decreased considerably. In fact, attention spans have plummeted from 12 seconds (Millennials) to 8 seconds (Generation Z).[27]

As a marketer, you know how important it is to capture attention. Well, unfortunately, this just got harder. Though, to be fair, the deluge of information that caused their brains to shift in the first place likely included your company's social media posts and sponsored ads to begin with.

However, there is hope for you yet, my marketer friends. As it turns out, members of this young generation can hyper-focus once they decide they are interested in something. More to come on that—I guarantee that this is going to change your marketing outlook and shift your strategic goals to a slightly new metric.

5 TAKEAWAYS FOR MARKETERS

1. **Offer choice:** Generation Z is more independent than generations that have come before. For a marketer, it will be important to give Generation Z choices to find inspiration, and opportunities to control how their experience is personalized.

2. **Align your brand with values of hard work and career advancement:** A recession mindset has led to some serious hustle among Generation Z. This group spends time envisioning a future career then takes immediate action to meet their goals. Associate your brand with values of hard work, stories of inspiring entrepreneurs who have succeeded by using your product or service, and learning new skills for their future.

3. **Speed and convenience:** Generation Z has grown up with constant connection, and in an unprecedented time of emerging tech: cars that auto-adjust speed and stay in their lanes; drones that deliver products to our doors; robots carry lunch to the office; same-day delivery. This has fundamentally changed their perception of convenience, and they expect a lot more from your business. This creates opportunities for marketers to explore new channels.

4. **Frictionless experience:** For brands today, loyalty is tougher than ever to earn and depends in large part on seamless (or even invisible) technological integration. In large part, this is what creates silky-smooth customer experiences.

5. **Shift your strategy toward capturing attention:** This generation is flooded with visual stimuli and processes it more rapidly than ever before. Will your ad be dismissed as noise, or will it connect with your audience? As marketers, we must be more strategic in terms of how we capture attention, or we will see a lot of wasted money on social media campaigns that do not stick with this audience.

X Gen Z is independent

X Gen Z builds their career constantly

X Gen Z expects everything at the tip of their fingertips

X Have to make your ads worth their time

PART II: THE TRENDS THAT MATTER

When I first met Cabe, a 20-year-old car enthusiast, he was telling me about how he fell in love with cars—hard. He shook his head and averted his eyes as he muttered about what first sparked his excitement in cars, knowing full well how it might sound to an outsider. It was, after all, the *Fast and Furious* movies, "as cliche as it sounds," he couched, that made him fall in love cars. He then did what he always does when he's bored or waiting or procrastinating or longing connection or just plain hungry: he opened Instagram. Post after post after post were all cars. Nearly every single post. This kid was not kidding when he said he was into cars. Occasionally there was a motorcycle, but that was the extent of the variation on his page.

This session happened early in our study, and at this time, I had never in my life seen such focused curation. I was in awe. I asked Cabe about it, and he explained how it was intentionally curated: "I follow multiple companies, groups, people. There's posts on here for events… different people's cars for sale. Basically, anything you could think about in the automotive culture, you can find on here, in my Instagram feed."

"How often do you use Instagram?" I asked. I wanted to know how long this took, how many hours a day had this young man been scrolling and following and unfollowing and curating this page to get it to this level.

He said he did not use it that much, maybe a couple times a day. He saw himself as a casual Instagram user. Later in the interview, as we mapped out a day in the life of Cabe, he discussed slightly different usage patterns: more like a couple of times an hour.

When it comes to Instagram, Cabe is not looking for anything specific; he is looking to be inspired. He is scrolling, waiting to find that special something to spark an interest so he can dive deeply into it. "I'm just looking," he says. And it is not for anything in particular. He wants to know what he *should* be interested in. He wants to see what's new, what people are talking about, and what people are doing. Moreover, it is far more social than one might think: he follows national and local car enthusiasts. He also follows brands, but he prefers following personalities. He does not post much himself: once a week he may toss up a photo of his aftermarket work on his car, or if he goes to a car show, he might post pics from there. He is more of a consumer and curator than contributor.

Even with just a couple photos a week and a few comments on other people's posts though—"the basics" he calls it—Cabe has built a substantial following for himself and his personal car-lover brand. He does not think much of the size of his following, which is just under 1,000. But that 1,000 mark is huge. Companies today are looking for nanoinfluencers at that level who are easy to deal with and who will endorse their products in an authentic way for a tiny commission. He does not see himself as an influencer in any way though: he says he clicks the like button on posts, and every so often adds comments, "You know, just the basics [to] see what people do, what they're doing." But what he *is* doing is more than "just the basics".

Cabe is, without realizing it, making sure he is a part of all the local car conversations going on in his city. It is on these posts that he tends to comment, and he is actively engaging in a community that he has helped foster. He is organically growing his brand and his following—as a creator—without even giving it a thought. It is natural and automatic.

As he scrolled, a sponsored ad caught his attention and he paused to tell me why it made him cringe: "This is another big company. They're kind of a worldwide group. Been following them for a while [and I] get annoyed by all of the ads that really have nothing to do with anything I'm interested in."

Marketers: listen up. You have to know what your customers are interested in before pushing ads their way. You are investing a lot here; a little research ahead of time can really pay off. Just because someone is following you does not mean that they are interested in every product you sell or every service you offer. Targeting these ads to the right groups is essential.

He passed it with a dry look of disdain, then lit up with a different post: "This is actually the company that I purchase my wheels through!" He was delighted to pass on their story and he continued with gusto, "They're based out of California. They custom-build anything that you want for anybody, from anybody, any brand, basically anything you want, they can do." Clearly, this was the inspiration Cabe was looking for, and he began to go down a rabbit hole of seeing what this brand was up to lately, what cool projects they were working on and any photos and videos they had. This tiny spark led to a hyper-focused, high-engagement activity with a brand that would lead to increased loyalty and sharing.

These emotional moments were fascinating to me: micro-ups and micro-downs swinging as the eyeballs rolled across the screen. Yea! Nah. Yea! Nah… This never ending, fast-paced context switching all the way through the feed has got to be exhausting.

Later on in the interview, Cabe and I spoke about trust and source credibility. "How do you know what sources to trust?" I asked.

"As far as sources I trust," Cabe explained, "There's basically a few main sources. They're not sources, but I guess you would say pages. There's like really big pages, there's one called, let me see if I can pull it up... *Stance Nation*. They've got almost four million people that follow them! They're really big and they've been around for years. The stuff that they say and the things they post is really relevant, really up-and-coming. It's from all over the world."

Cabe's enthusiasm quickened as he followed each of the pages, telling me about influencers he followed, how he found them, and that special moment when he decides to trust or not trust a creator in a video based on what they're saying and how they say it. The more these influencers talk about a struggle or challenge—when they showcase some vulnerability or the "real" part of their personality—*that* is when people like Cabe pay attention. "You can't fake that," he explains. This generation (most of whom spend around 3 hours on YouTube each night) has watched so many videos over the course of their lifetime that they have a built-in barometer about what's real and what's staged or scripted. *users want real emotion*

This is the type of interview that marketing dreams are made of!

Through qualitative and quantitative research, coupled with research from other literature and sources, we have unwrapped a number of key trends that you as a marketer need to know about for your brand to survive in this brave new world.

The next several sections of this book will walk through the trends that should matter to you and your brand positioning, pricing, content strategy, social media plan, research plan, and so much more.

SPECIFIC AND DISCERNING CONTENT CURATORS

Ready for a pop quiz? Cover up the chapter heading and try to guess this answer...

What are kids ages 13-25 NOT thinking about?

A. Hollywood celebrities

B. Curating a personal brand

C. Goat yoga

wrong

The answer: A.

Is it what you expected? No? Well, let's begin this section by covering three things that today's youth are NOT thinking about:

1. They are not thinking about Hollywood celebrities. Now, Instagram celebrities and YouTube celebrities... that's a different story.

2. They are not thinking about what they missed out on, like the magic of a single landline phone growing up and what it was like to fight with their family over talking to boys on the phone all night (don't act like you don't remember that!)

3. They are definitely not thinking about a bunch of marketers reading this book, trying to learn how to connect with them.

But that leaves a whole lot of things they *are* thinking about, and **curating their personal brand** is at the top of the list.

Members of this generation are also definitely thinking about goat yoga. Wait, don't tell me you have never heard of goat yoga? Bruh, let me explain. Goat yoga is a fad right now for 16-24 year olds. It is a yoga class in a room or outdoor area with pygmy goats that jump all over you while you get into yoga poses. Seriously. What's more, they tell you to bring a change of clothes because you will be peed or pooped on. If we are being honest here, I feel that with any amount of pee or pop involved, it should be in the title. But then again, I suppose a campaign for "poop yoga" would catch some attention but would probably not sell many tickets!

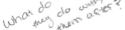

Photo Credit: CBS 13 News, https://www.youtube.com/watch?v=gvj6voiH5S0

Sidebar over. Let's get back to business and talk about one of the most important (and also one of the most consistent) findings from any study we have done with this age group: curation.

Many have labeled Millennials as a self-absorbed "Me" generation. In his book *The Narcissist Next Door: Understanding the Monster in Your Family, in Your Office, in Your Bed—in Your World*, author and *Time* editor Jeffrey Kluger argues, "Plenty of people are narcissistic in our society, but Millennials are doing these things on a pandemic level."

I would argue that this generation, which came of age with selfies and MySpace and Facebook and the Kardashians, was probably just trying to figure out social media for themselves. Yet, regardless of the psychology behind why Millennials share, the point is that they do. They share. A lot. Again. And again. And—OMG did you really eat avocado toast at brunch today?

We know that Millennials overshare. They know it too. On top of that, the false sense of authenticity they get from oversharing actually results in fewer closer connections. But here is where things get interesting. If Millennials are the generation of oversharing, Generation Z is the generation of painstaking curation. Generation Z is a group keenly aware of their digital legacy. They carefully curate and segment personal brands on social media, and for their unfiltered, uncultivated thoughts, they rely on apps that do not store data forever like Snapchat. Even as I write this, competitors are realizing they cannot match the benefits offered by Snapchat to Generation Z: Facebook CEO Mark Zuckerberg recently announced he would give Facebook and Instagram users more control over how long messages, posts, and photos exist. This includes an option that users can choose to make messages they send instantly disappear after being viewed or after a set amount of time—which sounds eerily similar to its rival Snapchat.[28]

✳ always thinking of who may be watching

Generation Z is made up of careful, discerning curators. Today's teens and young adults see their accounts as their personal brands, and select different content for different profiles and different platforms. While a 2017 study reported that 55 percent manage at least 2 Instagram accounts, my experience that is it not uncommon to see this age group with 4 or 5 Instagram accounts.

One teen, Libby, stood out in our interviews because she so articulately described the differences between her five Instagram accounts, and when and why she would switch between each. I met Libby for an interview in her family's home in Florida. The walls were filled with a combination of geometric art and posed portrait photos of she and her sisters that reminded me of the Sears variety that my mother used to drag my brother and me to once every few years. Her living room was cozy, with tan walls and oversized furniture. She was dressed in shorts and a baggy sweatshirt. On a plush, well-worn sectional sofa, she leaned back, phone in hand, and walked me through her Instagram profiles.

Before we dive into Libby's Instagram presence, I think it is important to know a little about the girl. This 16-year-old is smart and artistic with a dry sense of humor. She loves math and storyline gaming. Her hair is frizzy and she does not wear makeup. She might for Junior Prom, maybe some lipstick. She told me that sometimes she wears glasses to school (even though she sees 20/20) to make herself look more intelligent, to fit a persona she wants to embody: the smart, quiet introvert; the secret comedian; the future documentarian who stalks the halls of the school, invisible, observing every person and every angle.

When she opened Instagram, it immediately went to an account that she referred to as her "spam account." She even labeled it that way, with her user name followed by _spam. The description contained a joke about spam in a jar. She explained to me that this first o Will the age range change for GenZ over the years?

account was for "basically anything that I want to post... a place where I can see what my friends are doing." She paused, chuckling at a video that zoomed in on one of her high school friends, slumped over a desk, asleep in class. She pointed out that she did not have many followers here, only 39, but that was intentional. She did not want people to know the private moments in her life: "I don't have a lot of people on here 'cause it's strictly for my friends and it's so that I can post, you know, like whatever I want." She made fun of her older sisters for oversharing and sneered at their Millennial drama and shook her head at their risky online behavior with no attention to their privacy settings. She continued to scroll through her account, telling me about bits and pieces. She referred to it as "my main account" and noted the mish-mash of content from friends, YouTube personalities, and (of course) the occasional prom dress that she quickly zoomed by, almost embarrassed to look.

Then she said the most amazing thing: "This is where I post the good parts."

The good parts. Her spam account, the one that she said is for her to privately post anything she wants, is for "the good parts." Even in this safe, friends-only space, Libby spends time pulling and editing only the photos that portray her as the artist that she is. She scripts, films, edits, and posts short artistic videos. She gets her friends to perform in them. Only 39 people see these masterpieces, but her page is culled and curated with on-brand images and videos that would make her friends laugh or would show off just the witty and artistic and unique personality traits that she wants to project about herself and her individuality.

Her second account was a fan account for a YouTube influencer named Cody Ko, a Canadian-American comedian who got his start on Vine and then jumped platforms. She actually discovered him on

Vine and followed him. "So of course," she said, "I follow Cody Ko and friends." I mean, who doesn't?

"And then we have my photography account," she continued, toggling down to her next account. "You can consider it like a business." This girl is just 16 years old and is working to build a social media presence for her business! On this account, she posts her own photos and follows inspirational photographers and photography accounts that speckle her feed with images that speak to her. On days when she feels like she needs a dose of inspiration, she submerges herself here, in this account.

Lastly, Libby showed me an old account that she (yes, she admits) still checks every once in a while, an old fan page of… One Direction. On this page, she follows other One Direction fan pages to get the very latest on whether or not the band will ever get back together. I don't know about you, but I'm on pins and needles too.

"And yeah. That's it. Cool Cool," she ended her explanation, pausing expectantly while she awaited more of my questions.

When asked why she created all these accounts, she actually seemed a bit stumped. She did not quite understand what I was asking. I rephrased: "Why not just have one?" I don't recall for sure, but there may have been an eye roll. Ugh, these old people in their 30s just don't get it! It was totally natural for Libby to segregate different types of content into different buckets. In fact, it was the only way she seemed to be able to process the information. Later, we will talk a bit more about how teens today are natural aggregators themselves, and I hope you will remember this story when we do (if not, I'll remind you).

The key point here is that Libby, as well as the rest of her Generation Z cohort, is intuitively segmenting and curating personal brands. Grouping interesting content into different accounts on

Instagram, different boards on Pinterest, or any other means of categorization just feels right. It is something that to Generation Z is naturally understood, untaught, instinctual. Not only that, in switching between accounts, I have never seen fingers so fast. It is automatic, habitual, a route movement that makes me wonder if their fingers sweeping across the screen may move faster than they can process the data they are seeing. To Generation Z, when things are different, you group them, whether that's a list, a collection on Instagram, a board on Pinterest, or (in LIbby's case) a profile in Instagram. To this youth audience, it is the only way to make sense out of all the data inputs flying their way at any given moment.

For several years we have been reading articles on the difference between "finstas" and "rinstas" that explain how youth are creating an unfiltered Instagram account for a small group of friends ("real insta" or "rinsta") as well as a cultivated public persona (their "fake Insta" or "finsta").[29] However, in watching hundreds of kids use Instagram over the past year, I did not observe this trend.

What I did find was that nearly every account created and maintained by a young person was at least to some degree cultivated. Even when they reportedly posted everything about their lives, when you really dig into it, they didn't. Not on Instagram anyway. Posting anything is for Snapchat, where they know that their messages and photos will not live forever, reemerging years later to haunt them when they try to get a job or run for a political office. This is one of the reasons we couple quantitative survey data with deep qualitative interviews: often people say one thing and do another, and that is true even for youth. For Libby, even her most raw "rinsta", the account she called "spam… for posting everything and anything," ended up only for "the good parts".

I'm sure you are wondering at this point: how did it become so intuitive for Generation Z to process and curate information? The rest of us get overwhelmed and shut down with too much stimuli; these kids just take care of it. To answer this question, let's take a trip back to 2007, the year that the iPhone was released. At this time, the oldest members of Generation Z had yet to hit puberty and the youngest were still in diapers. Earlier in this book, we discussed how having high-speed Internet at home in high school was one of the defining characteristics that altered behavior, attitudes, beliefs, and values between Generation X and Millennials.

Similarly, for Generation Z, the introduction of the iPhone changed everything too.

Generation Z grew up with the iPhone. They grew up with unlimited information just a tap and swipe away. They grew up without a pause, where there was no time to think, but rather, just react. With the rise of social media, they were always "on", ready to respond, react, and comment on every moment for hundreds of friends and acquaintances—all of whom were suddenly within constant mental reach. According to a study out of the University of Texas at Austin, having a smartphone around constantly occupies and exercises a part of your brain, even unconsciously.[30]

This omnipresent force conditioned Generation Z to handle massive amounts of visual stimuli. Studies have even suggested that their brains have evolved to process more information, at faster speeds, than the rest of us.[31]

Where To Post And Where To Seek

While Millennials tend to cast a wide net when posting, putting the same content on multiple platforms, Generation Z is able to clearly articulate the distinction between when to use each social app. They intuitively understand where to post different types of content, and where to go to find specific types of content. This group mindfully chooses one location over another.

Here is how Generation Z feels about some of the most popular apps:

- **Instagram** = random inspiration, aspirational slice-of-life, edited
- **Pinterest** = inspiration in a specific area, like cake decorating
- **YouTube** = how-to's, DIY, learning something
- **Snapchat** = chatting with friends for fun, behind-the-scenes footage, raw
- **Twitter** = news, professional announcements (e.g., when a YouTuber has an event)
- **Google** = looking up specific facts, especially homework
- **Text message** = chatting with friends when important or timely (e.g., where to meet, homework questions)
- **GroupMe** = group chatting mainly among college students, and only the U.S. (everywhere else in the world uses WhatsApp)
- **Reddit** = gaming, long discussions
- **Facebook** = parents

Just a note about Facebook usage, and it is quite sweet really. When thinking about when Generation Z uses Facebook, it is in large part for communicating with their parents and often slightly older family members as well, for sharing a makeup video with a sister in college or for commenting on Mom's latest cat photo. When we do see Generation Z engaging in Facebook outside of a familial connection, it is typically when they have a hobby that is shared by those who typically skew older. For instance, a teenager interested in cars might join a group on Facebook to find out more about local car shows.

Generation Z will expect brands to abide by the rules of what content goes on what platform. Now I understand that social media management tools like Hootsuite and Buffer make it easy to share everything everywhere, but if you choose to blast the same copy on multiple platforms, it will not only annoy but also offend your Generation Z audience. Content should be at least slightly different, tailored for each tool.

Discerning About Devices And Apps

If you are a member of Generation Z, your phone is your temple.

More than likely, it is an iPhone. That means you text with a blue bubble, thank goodness. Let's talk about the green bubble for a moment, though, because I was blown away by what I saw. 82 percent of today's teens have iPhones, and Android users are social pariahs in this generation's version of mean girls.[32] Teens with blue bubbles respond less frequently to green. Android users are called "weird" in schools. Test and retest your content on iPhones: it is absolutely what matters in the United States.

App layout is equally important. Popular now: minimal apps on the home screen and dock; color coding; emojis to label folders; YouTube organization tutorials.

In looking at the screens of hundreds of teens' phones, we noticed something interesting: they very are specific about where to go (what app to use when), and they also keep their home screens (and docs) edited as well. Many times, we noticed just 2-4 apps total on the home screen and/or just 2-3 in the dock. This minimalist home screen organization could possibly be a reaction to the deluge of information coming their way: a calming response designed to counter the chaos of their social media lives.

Another popular organizational trend right now is color coding to organize apps, as well as adding emojis to folders. For instance, all apps with blue logos on them might be put into a folder with blue whale emojis, all apps with orange logos might be categorized into a folder with jack-o-lanterns, and so on. Organizing your phone and talking about how you organized your phone has become such a trend that there are channels on YouTube dedicated to phone organization tutorials.

Again, a pattern forms: Generation Z is desperately trying to build structure from chaos. Generation Z sorts, organizes, and categorizes naturally, automatically, intuitively.

The average 13- to 24-year-old checks social media about 100 times a day, and sends at least 8 snaps a day on Snapchat, to the point where the vocabulary blurs and they commonly call snapping "texting."[33]

5 TAKEAWAYS FOR MARKETERS

1. **The riches are in the niches:** Make sure that your social accounts are highly curated and your ads extremely specific and targeted so that people can tell what your brand is about in 8 seconds or less. As one of my favorite podcasters Pat Flynn says: "The riches are in the niches."

2. **Be a part of the conversation:** Generation Z spends a great deal of time and energy posting to their curated accounts and following similar accounts. If you want to organically grow your following of people who are highly engaged in a specific topic, you have to become a part of the conversation. Find accounts with whom your brand might be a good fit, and start to like posts and add comments. Engage with your followers, follow up on replies, and you will become a part of the conversation. Stay in the loop

3. **Make the scavenger hunt real:** Once your brand is noticed, you must have sufficient content in enough different places to make the scavenger hunt real. If you go through the hurdles of getting your brand noticed, you must provide enough content for someone to research and find you.

4. **Be selective about where you post:** Generation Z has its own rules of etiquette when it comes to where to post different types of content. You'll look like a novice (or worse yet, a Millennial!) if you post everything everywhere. I know it is tempting when you are using social media management tools that make it is so easy. But resist the urge.

5. **Deliver personalization:** Generation Z demands personalized experiences. They have no qualms about giving out their personal information to a profile in exchange for the promise of a more cultivated experience. To optimize your customer experience, ask your customers questions about their preferences. Conduct ongoing research to find out who they are, what segments they want to personalize for, and then do it.

X Don't post everything at once
X Don't post the wrong thing on the wrong platform

SNAP JUDGMENT, THEN DEEP DIVE

A "Niagara Falls" of information is beating down on Generation Z, every moment of every day. For this generation, it is nothing new and as a result, their brains have evolved to process inputs quicker than ever before.[34]

There is a video I like to show at conferences. It has no volume; it is just a recording of a teenager scrolling through the Explore section of Snapchat during a mobile diary study entry. It shows what she was doing in that precise moment in time. The clip is only 30 seconds long, but it is enough to make your head spin. Every time I watch it, I feel dizzy. In one section, the teen scrolls so fast that the images have not even loaded yet. Impatient or bored or maybe just out of habit, she keeps scrolling anyway.

The statistics say that on average, Generation Z has an 8-second attention span.[35] However, that is only 8 seconds once you have succeeded in catching their attention in the first place.

This generation is making gut decisions about what interests them, not in a matter of seconds—more like nanoseconds. Once they decide that something is interesting or worth their time, they click and for about 8 seconds, will focus on the pictures, watch a few seconds of video, or maybe even scan some text. That is a good 4 seconds less than people 25-35 years old.

It is harder than ever before to stand out.

Attention is not the same thing as engagement though, and if you think it is hard to be noticed in today's whirlwind of social media content, just try for something more: engagement.

Death Of Email?

In the past few years, social media engagement rates have dropped substantially. Rand Fishkin, former founder and CEO of Moz and a leader in the field of search engine optimization, recently shared a chilling study that revealed plummeting engagement rates. His comments here echo what many of us are feeling about the value of advertising on social media: the future outlook is not so great: "For most businesses," he says in a LinkedIn post in March 2019, "it's literally better to have ONE email subscriber than ONE THOUSAND likes on your Facebook page."

Sarah Weise commented on this   • • •

 Rand Fishkin • 1st
Author: Lost and Founder (out now!), Founder of SparkToro (prev Moz)
1w • Edited

My god... I had no idea social media engagement rates had dropped THIS low. A few years ago, we moaned about <5%, then <2%, but in 2019... we're seeing <0.1%!
Facebook: 0.09%
Instagram: 1.60%
Twitter: 0.048%
For most businesses, it's literally better to have ONE email subscriber than ONE THOUSAND likes on your Facebook page.
(source: Rival IQ's 2019 Social Media Industry Benchmarks - https://lnkd.in/gKyKEHe)

In a world where Generation Z uses so much social media for digital communications, as marketers we often tend to ignore email or assume that it is dying. Time and again, Generation Z studies debunk this myth. While they may not spend hours a day looking at email (they generally try to check it and get out as quick as possible), email is still a strong marketing channel and highly utilized even by younger generations. In fact, 85 percent of Generation Z cite an "overwhelming preference" for email as a communication channel. That is slightly lower than we have seen in the past: 89 percent of Millennials and 92 percent Generation X answers in the same way.[36]

At this time, Generation Z is less likely to use email for work than previous generations, relying more on text messages. Since most of Generation Z right now is too young to have a full-time job, I would expect email usage to increase for them in future years. Right now, 7 in 10 use email for communication with their friends. 7 in 10 also open messages from companies (ads, coupons, receipts, and password resets). But only 1 in 3 use emails to communicate with co-workers, and only 1 in 4 used email to communicate with companies associated with their occupation.[37]

The engagement numbers on social media are not great because there is so much noise out there. That is precisely why Generation Z has adapted, with much faster scroll speeds. They scroll 2.5 times as fast as Millennials![38] Many advertisers want a guarantee that their social media ads will be seen for X number of seconds. However, this is not an effective metric because by that measure, you are basically weighing older viewers' attention more than younger viewers' attention.

This is one of the reasons that Facebook ads have gone to *relative* scroll times. For a specific person, Facebook can measure how fast they typically scroll, and knows if a specific ad was noticed based on whether there was a discernible slowing of the scroll. The time paused is different for each person, but relative. That means that if you are advertising on social media, do not expect to use the number of seconds your ad was viewed as a reliable metric. A better metric is a relative measure of attention: how many people slowed enough over your ad to pay attention to it.

Big Opportunity For Engagement (If You Can Capture Attention)

Just when you thought things were looking real hopeless, consider this: the moment Generation Z decides they are interested in a story or a personality, they go nuts.

I mean, really nuts.

Do not crumple up that social media strategy just yet because if you can capture their attention, a switch flips and they turn into mini-stalkers (and I do mean that in the most endearing way). These youth deep dive into what sparked their interest, searching for every shred of information they can find and seek out exclusive information, hidden secrets.

The harder it is to find, the greater the gratification.

The quirkier the better.

"Can you believe [insert personality here] hates ranch dressing? Who in their right mind hates ranch dressing?"

Generation Z wants to know everything about the people they follow, whether a niche musician or a YouTube celebrity. They crave the behind-the-scenes story, and want to know about authentic and personal insights into their lives.

They expect photos, stories, trips, fashion—at all hours of the day. Instagram provides the aspirational slice-of-life exhibition they crave. But they use at least 2 to 3 other apps or sites to find fresh, different information. Given the fact that they do not read nearly as much as past generations, is really incredible how good these kids are at online research and finding out things about a particular interest, a band they like ora YouTuber they follow. In large part, it is because they are willing to spend the time doing it. They will watch every YouTube video their favorite creator ever made, find out her age, significant other, family, friends, where she lives, personal details of her life and become super-fans on Instagram and Snapchat and Twitter and anywhere else. So, just know that you will need to serve up content that meets this need. Once they love you, you need to keep the content love affair going!

I want to tell you a story of an ethnographic study I did with a 17-year-old named Garrett. I walked into his home, a spotless single family home in a small suburb of a large city. It was a small rambler with great light and a hot tub in a postage-stamp size backyard. It was meticulously clean: not a fingerprint on a window, not a speck of dust on the television.

Garrett was a unique kid. He was into hunting and acoustic guitar. He aspired to go into the military like his father before him, and he had rock & roll music deep in his soul. We sat in his living room, which was an open concept that connected to the kitchen. I gazed around and noticed that from corner to corner, every tiny little nook and cranny had something decorative in it. Every wall was covered with motivational phrases in gold cursive fonts. Framed prints and shadow boxes with fabric pinned in them hung daintily anywhere there was even a tiny bit of white space. Every table had a color-coordinated chatchkee. There was a set of matching tea cups on one, with a cursive monogram on each for every member of the household. It looked like Home Goods and Etsy had gotten together and had a love child.

Garrett looked out of place and awkward in this meticulously cared for home. He was sitting on a black kitchen chair that had been set in the living room before we arrived. He had clearly been asked by his parents to wear a collared shirt. It looked new and itchy. His back was as straight as could be against the wooden chair, and he seemed like he couldn't quite get comfortable. But he said he liked it there, and he wanted to stay.

The contextual interview started and Garrett was fairly guarded at first. That is, until we started talking about music. I asked what kind of music he liked, and he leapt up with a quickness, ushering us into his bedroom where his guitar was. It was out already, tossed across his bed. He had been playing it before we knocked on the door. His room was cozy, just big enough for a double bed, desk and guitar stand. On his desk sat an Amazon Echo, and he asked Alexa to play. He immediately recognized the song as something he had heard before, and paused our interview to look up the artist.

It turned out it was a band called Carpenter Brut. We followed his lead and observed what he would have done if we had not been there. What he did astounded us. This teenage boy proceeded to spend the better part of 90 minutes finding out everything there was to know about this band, Carpenter Brut. All because he heard an intro of a song and it sparked his interest.

As he scoured the Internet in search of anything related to the band, he explained that he was, "Just finding little tidbits of information I could use."

"What will you use the information for?" I asked.

"Keep up with him… following [him]… just listening."

Garrett explained that he had been listening to this genre of music quite a bit recently, including several other vaporwave or retrowave artists. The fact that Carpenter Brut just seemed to "pop up" was fortuitous, but Garrett knew that it was informed by his past listening activity. Sharing listen history with companies like Spotify,

Amazon, Google, or Apple did not phase Garrett in any way. On the contrary, he assumed these companies were taking the data in order to make better, more personalized experiences for him. He wanted to share, and he appreciated that the personalization was "so me."

For Garrett, the first stop was his Spotify account, where he was able to see recent albums, upcoming tours, popular songs, and related artists. One by one, he looked into all the other albums, any singles, everything he could find. He said he was going through this to, "Just make sure I'm with it."

After Spotify, Garrett bounced to Sound Cloud. He was delighted that he could see more personal information about the artist, and dig into his life by learning things that he likes. He pointed out that there was less content here than on Spotify, but it was slightly different content, more "posts and anything that he likes".

After that he went to BandCamp on Safari, the artist's Facebook page, his personal website, YouTube, Instagram, and Twitter. On BandCamp, he felt like he could support Carpenter Brut. A number of online sites gave him tour dates and locations. But the most interesting interaction was on YouTube. "I can find the tracks or songs on Spotify, Sound Cloud, or his website. [YouTube is for] trailers or teasers or just separate videos using his music that he's just part of. If he posts a status, that's also helpful. [I want to know] anything related to him… that's just not anywhere else."

I asked how he knew whether or not he could trust these sources. He knew he could because, "They are the easiest things that I could just think of—they're accessible. They're just simplistic and just there, ready to be used, just on the fly." The idea of trust for Garrett was about ease of use, accessibility, and new information.

What struck the researchers in the room most was that even though Garrett was seeing a ton of repeated information, he kept looking. With just a spark of interest, this kid was able to hyper-focus for almost 90 minutes, and even though he kept seeing the same information, he kept digging. And oh my goodness—after 60 minutes of looking, when he found a new little tidbit about the artist's life, he went nuts. I don't remember what it was—probably the type of salad dressing this musician liked—but it didn't matter. What he was looking for was fresh info. He was on a mission, a scavenger hunt across the Internet to find something new, something that piqued his interests yet again.

I circled back with Garrett after the interview, and he said that after we left, he had listened to every album and every song by Carpenter Brut. He watched every YouTube video, every interview, anything he could get his eyes on.

The moral of this story, for you my marketer friend, is that for Generation Z especially, it is hard to capture attention. But once you do, good golly lights and sirens! These kids are amazing. Unlike constantly-distracted Millennials, Generation Z can tune everything else out in order to focus and learn—and they will be excited to do so!

So find a way to grab their attention and get them interested. Once you do, do not share everything on every platform. You will literally be able to manufacture delight each time something fresh and new is discovered, so scatter tidbits from place to place in order to make the scavenger hunt real. This keeps them focusing, keeps them going down the rabbit hole, keeps them interested in you and your brand.

5 TAKEAWAYS FOR MARKETERS

1. **Want engagement? Focus first on attention:** It is incredibly difficult to consistently capture attention of a Generation Z audience. If you can get past this and spark their attention, you will be rewarded handsomely, with hours and hours of incredibly focused, stalker-style engagement.

2. **Generation Z scrolls so, so fast:** Just because they scrolled by your ad doesn't mean they did not see it. This generation scrolls so much faster than Millennials and older generations that Facebook and Instagram now measure relative scroll speeds to measure attention (as they should). Don't be concerned if your ads are getting less minutes of view time with this generation: it does not mean their attention is less; it just means they may scroll faster.

3. **Piggyback off an existing interest:** To increase the chance of being noticed in a noisy world, tap into what your audience is already interested in. Get to know your customers and develop personas that clearly outline related interests.

4. **Quality content wins every time:** Quality content is still the name of the game for Generation Z. Even better: it does not have to be fresh content. They are just

as interested in evergreen articles, especially related to skill-based learning, as long as they are still relevant.

5. **Email is not dead:** Social media has an opportunity for better, bigger engagement than email. While an email will never go "viral", it is an effective communication strategy because it is routinely used by Generation Z. It should be combined as a part of an integrated marketing strategy for a consistent base of awareness and (if relevant) e-commerce.

X Just because they see, it doesn't mean they care. Just b/c they pay attention, It doesn't mean they're engaged.

X Find your target audience and research their current interests

INSPIRATION COMES IN THE FORM OF PERSONALIZED FEEDS

Like many in Generation Z, Anika found herself on Instagram all the time. She said she was not specifically looking for anything; it was just out of habit. Whenever she had a free moment, she pulled out her phone and went to Instagram. She might go to other apps, but Instagram was always where she started.

When she talked about this app, she used a term that many others in Generation Z use to describe why they come: "inspiration".

> I'll open it and go immediately to the Discovery page just to see what inspiration I can get or what things I can find new on here.

> Instagram offers me like a lot of inspiration as far as cooking or fashion, just because it will offer me random things that are related to topics that I'm already either searching or based on people that I follow specifically.

She talked about the differences between searching and browsing:

> Compared to a search engine, you know, a search engine can do that. It closes the chance of, you know, having random things selected for you, and the connections between things, because it gives you precisely what you want, versus

Instagram I can scroll and scroll and scroll for hours just looking at new content.

For a marketer, what is essential to know here is that inspiration comes in the form of personalized feeds. For Generation Z, scrolling is inspiring. It opens the door to let sparks of excitement in, and Generation Z comes here desperate to catch and cling on to one of these sparks.

When browsing on a feed, Generation Z expect deeply personalized recommendations. They spend hours scrolling through feeds, looking for something that speaks to them. While it may appear mindless, it is actually the primary way youth seek out inspiration. For generation Z, the main purpose of scrolling is for inspiration.

While there is always a chance of inspiration from scrolling, it can often feel flat. For an average of 3 hours a day, teens scroll and scroll and scroll and wait and wait and wait until something catches their eye.[39] There is a term for this called "phone boredom". Yes, I'm aware that this term is extremely creative. Phone boredom occurs when you are technically on your phone, but you are still bored.[40]

Older generations see youth on their phones and assume that this entertainment is indefinite, yet phones do not always "offer salvation from the type of mind-numbing boredom that is so core to the teen experience."[41] When Generation Z is "phone bored," what they are doing is waiting for inspiration, mindlessly clicking around, scrolling forever, opening and closing apps, and ultimately just looking for something that sparks an interest but finding the options unsatisfying.

Whereas previous generations may have flicked through countless TV channels, today's teens systematically open and close up to 30 apps at a time, hoping that something, anything, will catch their attention.[42] However, from a Generation Z perspective, all of this scrolling is worth it. The feeling of being inspired or learning something new is so positive and necessary that they will spend a great deal of time trying to reproduce that sensation, scrolling to find that special something that speaks to them. *Even if they are bored from scrolling, they will continue to do so.*

For Anika, phone boredom does not last long when she is on Instagram, because Instagram is highly personalized to what she likes:

> *Instagram knows what type of things I like because I've already either followed someone who's, you know, related to that topic or something that I've already clicked or already searched previously, and it tells me what I should know or what I want to... know. It'll kind of bring those things to the top as far as pages that I look at a lot it, it's right there. Boom, it's right at the top. And, you know, without me having to ask for specifically like I would in a search engine.*

While Generation Z is cautious about putting their personal information out there, they have no qualms about doing it when it will make an experience more tailored to their needs. For Anika and Garrett and many like them, Instagram's personalization is not creepy. It knows you because you *let* it know you. "It doesn't follow you around like a stalker," Anika explains, "You teach it what you like by following people, by clicking on things."

What seems a bit frightening to me is not how well the algorithms know you; that is engineering. What is slightly terrifying is the fact that this generation is dependent on them to find out what interests them. *They don't know themselves enough to do it on their own.*

When I started my first youth research project, I went back to Georgetown where I earned my MBA and where I still lecture a couple times a semester. I met with one of my former marketing professors, Luc Wathieu. Professor Wathieu is a Millennial expert, not just in terms of his research (though it is prolific) but also because he has 10 children (yes, 10!). I'll let him correct me if I'm wrong, but I believe at least a handful of them are Millennials. That said, he has had quite a bit of immersive experience to supplement his research: ethnography at its finest! What the Professor had to say really stuck with me, and it has proven to be true in nearly every research study I have done with teens and young adults since.

He believed that there has been a shift in the question that goes into a customer's mind. Older generations ask, "What *do* I want?" then go to a search engine and find it. But today's youth do not think in these terms. Millennials and Generation Z alike tend to ask, "What *should* I want?" then rely on scrolling through feeds to find inspiration.

Now, let's go back and look at what Anika said in her interview. She literally says that Instagram tells her what she "should" know and what she "wants" to know, without her having to ask:

> *Instagram knows what type of things I like because I've already either followed someone who's, you know, related to that topic or something that I've already clicked or already searched previously, and **it tells me what I should know or what I want to... know**. It'll kind of bring those things to the top as far as pages that I look at a lot it, it's right there. Boom, it's right at the top. And, you know, without me having to ask for specifically like I would in a search engine.*

What does this say about the shift in critical thinking in modern-day youth, that they rely on recommendation engines to tell them what to be inspired by or interested in? Or that they will scroll for hours, watch YouTube videos on auto-play, or open 30 different apps, just to find something that does not bore them to death? It makes me wonder if "inspiration" for this generation may be more tied to seeing something unexpected or learning something new than we previously thought.

As a parent of young children, I have to admit I often feel mortified when hear a participant in one of our studies tell me that they watch YouTube around 3 hours a day and spend even more hours scrolling through Instagram and gaming, "sometimes until 3am… yes, on a school night," one 17-year-old told me. It is terrifying—not just because of how screen usage is physically altering the brain—but also because our society's teenagers have stopped reading.

A 2019 Neisen study shows that teens perform worse than adults when completing tasks on websites for three reasons: (1) Insufficient reading skills; (2) Less sophisticated research strategies; (3) Dramatically lower levels of patience.[43] According to this report, teens were most successful on e-commerce sites because they all look fairly similar (what UX professionals call "following design patterns"), and also because they required little reading. These teens encountered the most difficulty on sites with dense content including government, non-profit, school sites. It makes me want to shake them and yell "BRAH—Pick up a book!"

One teen gamer named Ashley told me about how she finds new games to play. After searching for a game she likes on YouTube, she clicks the recommendations, one after another, watching playthroughs (i.e., videos of other kids playing the games):

> *YouTube is going to know what I'd like, more than I would on my own. Let's say I really enjoyed a game like 'The Last of Us.' I'd find a playthrough of a YouTuber I like playing it. From there, more post-apocalyptic games would pop up and I'd choose from the related options. I'd watch playthroughs and decide if one of them looks good. When people genuinely*

look like they're having fun playing a game, I start to think that I want to experience that fun too. It's an excitement… anticipation.

For Generation Z, there is a blurring between social usage and knowledge-finding. A search engine like Google is typically only used by Generation Z when they are looking up something specific that they need an answer to. It is not for inspiration; it is for completing homework.

Even young Millennials use search engines sizably more than Generation Z. When asked to find news headlines in one of our studies, for example, Millennials typically went to Google. Generation Z, however, almost all took to social media (Facebook, Snapchat, Twitter) to answer this question.

X They trust real reactions

5 TAKEAWAYS FOR MARKETERS

1. **Inspiration comes from feeds:** In the minds of Generation Z, the question has shifted from "What do I want" to "What should I want". This generational cohort relies on recommendation engines to feed them suggestions on what to be interested in. If you want to be top of mind, you need to show up on their social feeds.

2. **Aim for inspiration and learning:** On Instagram and YouTube, aim for inspiration and learning. On Snapchat, go for light-hearted fun. For email marketing, focus on conversions (get them to click that button!)

3. **Test to find out what ignites your customers:** Based on your customer research, you should know quite a bit about your target audience (if you don't, call me—we can fix that in no time!) But when you're working on a campaign, you may not know what sparks of inspiration will fly until you try it out. A/B test your campaigns and see what ignites your tribe.

4. **Focus on design:** Grabbing the attention of visual Generation Z consumers takes eye-catching graphic design on both social media posts and in video. Consumers respond favorably to branded content

that is authentic, well designed and relevant. Because social media is mostly visual for Generation Z, design plays a major role. When you look at influencers on Instagram, nearly all look professionally designed and managed by brand guidelines with specific colors and font choices.

5. **Deliver personalization:** Generation Z demands personalized experiences. While they are a more cautious generation when it comes to sharing posts, they do not hesitate to give out their personal information to a profile in exchange for the promise of a more cultivated experience. To optimize personalization of a customer's experience, ask questions about their preferences. Conduct ongoing research to find out who they are, what segments you want to personalize for, and do it.

CRAVING AUTHENTICITY AND THE REAL-LIFE STORY

Step aside, Hollywood celebrities. Generation Z couldn't care less about your drama. Unlike Millennial reality TV addicts who thrive on it, Generation Z wants to peer into the real, authentic lives of the people they follow online. They consistently state that they do not want drama or the uncertainty of knowing what is real and what is not. This is one of the reasons that Generation Z follows more YouTubers and Instagram personalities who obsessively post. To Generation Z, the slice-of-life story seems more authentic and real—even though they intuitively understand that these stories are edited and curated.

Have you noticed that I've been using the term "Hollywood Celebrities"? Just saying "Celebrity" is no longer enough because there are Hollywood Celebrities, Instagram Celebrities, YouTube Celebrities, Vine Celebrities, Myspace Celebrities, Livejournal Celebrities… Ok, maybe not the last couple, but I wanted to make sure you were still paying attention!

Generation Z respects self-made and local celebrities because what they have is attainable. They get inspired to do the same. They understand that these personalities are very much a business and make money for themselves. Becoming Insta-famous by playing video games or teaching makeup tips or documenting the aspirational jet-setting lifestyle seems like a super fun way to earn passive income, am I right?

This generation constantly thinks in terms of influence, and the fame and money that it might bring them. They are both infatuated with and tormented by the likes and clicks and the number of followers they would need to rise to the level of sponsorship. They obsess over it, even when they claim that it is no big deal. The tracking of likes and clicks can be addictive and disheartening, with dramatic emotional swings occurring in this younger generation as a result.

While a decade ago, Millennial teenagers used social media to update their statuses and to see what their friends were up to, Generation Z has a much different attitude for using. For this younger generation, social media is primarily seen as a hub for content consumption. In fact, Generation Z spends far more time using social media for learning and entertainment than they do to stay in touch with their friends.[44] This is a positive sign for brands like yours because it means that if you create great content and can get it in front of Generation Z, they will read/watch/listen to your content and engage with you—because that's what they are doing online anyway. Your brand can easily insert itself into this existing customer journey.

You might be amazed at how much time exactly Generation Z is spending on social media. While Millennials spend an average of 2 hours, 39 minutes on social media per day, Generation Z spends 3 hours on average.[45] On top of that, they are spending the bulk of this time on different apps, ones that are, as a whole, more visual. While Millennials are apt to be on Facebook and Twitter, Generation Z is spending their time on Instagram, YouTube, and Snapchat.

When marketing to Millennials, a direct brand-to-consumer approach is likely to be effective because Millennials tend to follow brands they like on social media and share their posts. Generation Z, on the other hand, is far more likely to follow people—personalities—on social media. To stay authentic for this audience, many brands have seen success with influencer marketing as their go-to strategy. These brands have found that in large part, influencer marketing beats direct brand interaction to engage Generation Z consumers because of its unobtrusive, snackable content that is naturally relevant to what followers of this Instagram or YouTube creator are expecting to see on their channel.[46] While 3 in 10 would share from a YouTuber, only 2 in 10 would share from a known brand.[47]

Brands like Airbnb, Snickers, Old Spice, and Totino's are already tapping into this opportunity, contracting influential streamers to host special segments on behalf of the brand. When influencers talk about brands, people listen. Take Kim Kardashian's photo of her $30M Airbnb accommodation.[48] If the Kardashians are down with Airbnb, you should be to.

Here is a quote from a 17-year-old interview participant who explains why she prefers to follow people rather than brands:

> I don't search for "makeup tutorials" on YouTube. I search up specific people who do makeup. For example, I might search for Alyssa Forever, I like her makeup videos. I would search her and see if she has any new videos. I'm subscribed to her. She doesn't just do makeup. She does "How to fix your clothes and make it into something else" or "Turn a sweater into a crop top" or something like that. Hair videos. So I follow people rather than topics. And I follow people who I find to be authentic.

There's that word again: authentic.

Even big names can make themselves seem within reach by tapping into this value of authenticity on social media. One 21-year-old participant told us why she follows Cardi B on social media:

> *[I follow] celebrities… if you wear cute clothes, if you do cool stuff, if you always are posting about things that I can relate to. I'm not gonna follow a celebrity who's always in name brand stuff that I can't afford or can't get access to. I don't really watch their pages much versus a celebrity [like] Cardi B. She wears Fashion Nova. I know when I see something that she has on, I can go on Fashionnova.com and literally buy the same thing she has on.*

There is so much that brands can learn from listening to their customers or potential customers talk about who and what they follow and why. Make sure your company has a robust research plan (if they don't, call me!).

What we are seeing is that the most effective brands are authentic in their posts or their sponsorship activities. They show personality and be real, select creators where there is a value-added relationship for the viewers. Above all, they ensure that the brand is within reach. If Cardi B can do it, you can too: her fashion line is realistic, not too good to be true, and above all, accessible.

The second thing we are seeing is that successful companies go to where their customers are already. If they know that their customer base is watching video after video of specific YouTube channels on autoplay, or searching Instagram for hashtags on niche content, this is a great start. They can then look into the journey of their customers and find the creators who are providing the right type of content, then choose the right influencers to sponsor.

Here is an example of a company who very literally went to where their customers were, and we are not talking social media. They went... to the toilet.

The Skimm is a pithy news publisher targeting Generation Z and young Millennials with short, snackable content (both text and audio). Their brand is one born of authenticity and dry humor. They found out that over 61 percent of Americans have used their phones in the bathroom, and 43 percent do it frequently. While in the bathroom, 30 percent will answer the phone, and 44 percent have heard a toilet flush while on the phone. 9 percent have actually dropped their phone in the toilet. Yuck. 49 percent who use their phones on the toilet send text messages and 92 percent check social media. 31 percent have stayed in the bathroom longer than necessary to finish whatever they are doing or reading on the phone.[49] Are all of these statistics really needed here? No, absolutely not. You get the idea. But the point is that as a result of their customer research, the company launched something new, funny, and successful (at least anecdotally) on their app: the 5-minute toilet read. It's genius if you think about it.

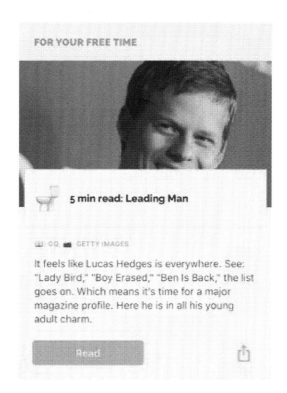

Not only is this seen as authentic and helpful for quick,

snackable learning in the way that it surfaces content, it is also funny and on-brand for this particular company.

Overall Generation Z is craving authenticity. If you can provide that effectively, especially through people and personalities that your audience already follows, your brand will be one step ahead of the game.

5 TAKEAWAYS FOR MARKETERS

1. **Social media as a hub for content consumption:**
   While Millennial teens primarily use social media to
   keep up with friends, Generation Z sees social media
   as a hub for content consumption. This is very good
   for brands like yours because it means that if you create great content and can get it in front of them, they
   will engage. Focus on creating quality content geared
   toward inspiration or learning.

2. **Value over ads:** Generation Z can smell salesy content from a mile away. Be honest, authentic, and show
   value to them—what will your product or brand do
   to enhance their lives? How will it help them make an
   impact?

3. **Be transparent:** Use honest, transparent, authentic
   messaging when talking with your customers, even if
   may feel vulnerable. Write in a conversational tone consistent with your brand personality, and post even when
   it is not great. Be real and above all, make sure your
   brand is within reach. If Cardi B can do it, you can too.
   accessible

4. **Go to where your customers are**: Find out what your
   specific audience does, and use that to your advantage. If you know that your customers are spending
   hours a day watching YouTube videos on gaming, go

to YouTube and either sponsor an influencer in that space or create complimentary, original content.

5. **Boost brand engagement with influencer marketing:** Partner with an Instagram or YouTube creator who will endorse your brand in an authentic way. Messages from influencers resonate over messages from brands. Look for nanoinfluencers with only 1,000 followers or more, especially if you have a local brand and they are a local personality. For a small commission, they may be willing to laud your product, and they tend be easier to deal with. Hiring multiple nanoinfluencers instead of relying on a single creator with a massive audience will make your brand seem like it is all over the place in a more authentic way. You will appear within reach for the everyday consumer, a value that Generation Z highly admires.

NATURAL AGGREGATORS OF INFORMATION

With unparalleled access to technology, Generation Z spends a tremendous amount of time on their phones. In fact, many had smartphones even in elementary school. According to TechCrunch, the average age at which a child receives their first phone is 10, but that statistic comes from 2016 so I would imagine it is slightly younger today.[50] Either way, the point is that teens are processing more information than ever before, at unprecedented rates. To make sense of the staggering amount of information these developing brains must process, Generation Z has become aggregators, collecting, grouping, and organizing everything—all the time.

These natural aggregators of information collect tabs, aggregated clippings of information, images, bookmarks, reading lists, and more. Remember Libby, the high school junior who had no less than 5 Instagram accounts? She collected and grouped different information into each Instagram account.

What does this mean for the future? This group is primed to become natural analysts, taking large amounts of information and breaking it down into smaller, more manageable groupings and chunks to make sense of it.

Here are a few ways that Generation Z groups and stores lists of information:

"My screenshot gallery is ridiculous"

"I text myself links"

"I love, love, love collecting bookmarks"

"I paste text from different sites into the Notes app"

"I'm a tab hoarder"

"I use Pinterest collections for inspiration"

Given the tendency toward aggregating and grouping, it is only natural that their minds would gravitate toward ready-made collections: Quizlet, Pinterest, Evernote, and more.

When talking about homework, Quizlet is one of the most revered apps because it enables students to list and study flashcards of information, and even has lists made by other students taking the same class (in their school or other schools). I suppose that brings new meaning to the term *social* studies. The reason this resonates with this group is because of the aggregation of information, as well as the ability to study from the phone.

Another tool we heard a lot about was Pinterest. Though Millennials typically use Pinterest more than Generation Z, we do see Generation Z opening it when they want inspiration on something specific. This app is appealing because its is designed for collections, and allows the consumer (or a group) the ability to co-create collections. While Instagram is perceived as the app for random inspiration, Pinterest is perceived as the app for inspiration on specific topics in a more tailored way. On Pinterest, I have watched Generation Z search for queries like these:

"goldish prom makeup"

"styling air max shoes"

"cake decorating"

"making slime"

"at-home ballet workouts"

"goat yoga"

It is worth noting that in our own studies, we exclusively observed females using Pinterest; Generation Z males hardly gave it a thought.

Instagram itself has taken the hint and moved more toward more categorized content. As illustrated below, when you save posts, you can add them to collections (a) which look eerily similar to pins from Pinterest. At the top of the Explore area, there are categorized buckets (b). Even on profile pages, Instagram story highlights enable an individual or brand to group their content to make it easier for their customers to see (take note, marketers, you should do this on your Instagram page if you have not already).

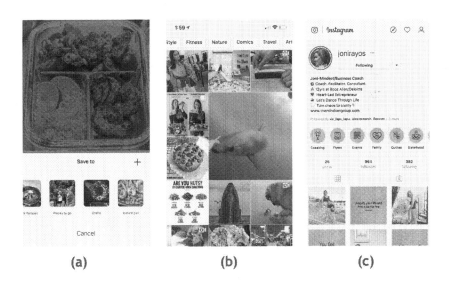

(a)   (b)   (c)

5 TAKEAWAYS FOR MARKETERS

1. **Encourage users to create collections:** Allow co-creation of lists and category groupings. Try contests on Instagram and/or Pinterest to encourage brand engagement with these natural aggregators.

2. **Add sharing to collections:** If you allow collections to be created by your users, make sure there is an easy way for them to share them with others. Sharing will be higher since the user feels a sense of ownership.

3. **Categorize your content based on interests:** Organize the content on your website or social media accounts for users as best you can. If you have a lot of content on your site, ask your users what they want to see. These categories, combined with personalization settings, will be much-appreciated by this generation. On Instagram, create story highlights to categorize the types of content you provide and give a viewer a reason to follow you. On Pinterest, create specific boards to match niche sub-categories.

4. **Use lists in your content creation:** Knowing that this generation loves lists and categories, regularly schedule lists and listicles in your content calendar. This can certainly be done in the form of blogs, but Generation Z might be more inclined to watch video.

5. **Get yourself on their camera roll:** Generation Z takes screenshots often. Screenshots are eternally saved on their phones and they often scroll through them when looking for something in particular that they saved. Create content that Generation Z would want to save or share (something worth taking a screenshot of), of course making sure that your design is beautiful and on-brand.

TIME OBSESSION FROM THE ON-DEMAND GENERATION

Generation Z is obsessed with time, schedules, and time management. Perhaps Generation Z is overscheduled, overworked, or overwhelmed. Perhaps this is in response to the deluge of information they are getting on a minute-to-minute basis. But whatever the cause, they think about time. A lot. They stay up late. They plan and scheme about how to be more productive or more efficient with their time. They imagine how to do things faster. Ionically, they spend lots of time looking for hacks to save little bits of time.

Expectation Of Speed

This is the first generation that has truly depended on on-demand services to be readily available as a part of their daily routines. When Millennials were teens, they had to wait for their parents to catch a ride. Generation Z has Uber and Lyft accounts. If they need food, it is just a couple clicks away. They do not even need to pick up the phone and talk with someone; they just order it on their phone and it comes to the door. If they are bored... Wait, what do you mean you old people used to daydream? Generation Z certainly does not have time for that—they are far too busy infinitely scrolling and constantly learning.

When it comes to transactions, this generation does not tolerate sluggishness. They expect speed and efficiency in everything they do. That is why if you are creating a user interface that is going to be used by Generation Z, your technology must be invisible, lightning-fast, with seamless transitions between disparate touchpoints—going on a website, using a mobile app, walking into a retail store, texting customer service for help. Of course, everything must also work flawlessly on mobile, and preferably in an app versus a mobile website. If Generation Z notices the technology, you're doing something wrong.

Make It Worth My Time

While food-based gluttony is Generation Z's vice of choice, sloth is the sin that they try to avoid most. As an entrepreneurial generation that grew up with unprecedented access to digital tools and information to help them learn, explore, and entertain themselves, Generation Z feels that there is no excuse to be idle or bored.

It is clear that Generation Z spends a lot of time on their phones. But based on what types of content they are consuming, they have a very different perspective on whether or not it was worth their time.

In general, Generation Z thinks of content in terms of three key buckets: inspiration (feeling motivated or interested, usually by example); education (learning something new); and entertainment (zoning out while binging on YouTube or Netflix). While they tend to associate the inspiring and educational content with positive emotions of empowerment, self-improvement, and excitement, they tend to associate content whose sole purpose it is to entertain with feelings of guilt because they know they could be spending their time more wisely.

Inspiring content motivates them to want to do something, create something, be active for a cause, or better themselves or their world in some way. The most inspiring content is through personal stories: influencers certainly, but also TED talks, interviews with role models, heart-wrenching stories on YouTube, and shareable quotes that "speak to me". Generation Z spends hours and hours scrolling through feeds waiting for this inspiration to strike. It is such a positive feeling that it is worth it to spend time trying to reproduce it.

Learning something new is also similar. This "something new" could be anything; it runs the gamut from how to improve my coding skills, how to beat this level in a game, how to apply powder foundation, how to learn guitar, how to cook, workout videos, details about exotic cars, how to improve my free throw, how to make a pom pom rug, how to cut a sweatshirt crop top, how to take better photos, how to solve a specific math equation, how to get sponsored by YouTube (remember, internet-famous is the new celebrity), how to write a great college essay, how to deal with a bully, or even how to get involved in stopping gun violence in schools.

YouTube videos are the primary source for this do-it-yourself (DIY) learning, though some topics (activism especially) might actually require a search. Notice that learning something new is not necessarily tied to what kids are doing in school—it is anything they believe will help them accomplish a goal in their life, hobbies, or future career, or anything else. Remember, Generation Z is progressive, efficient and (most of all) real.

Many of these learning videos are interactive, like lessons for coding, gaming, musical instruments, cooking, fitness. Generation Z takes their learning everywhere with them and often looks for help in the moment they need it, in the context they need it in, which is different from past generations. Additionally, expertise does not seem to be tied to research. This finding surprised me, given how much research this group does on just about any topic that catches their fancy. But this is a generation of doers, and they do not believe that you start becoming an expert until you consistently apply what you have learned, and practice it often. Teens may spend 2+ hours learning about something a night and still call themselves novices. I recently met a 14-year-old who loves makeup. She spends 3+ hours a day exploring beauty topics. She is captivated, engrossed, obsessed, and maybe even a little bewitched by James Charles. She watches every YouTube video, every Instagram post, and every behind-the-scenes snap. But she shared this insight: so does everybody else. I was expecting that she would rate herself an expert on this topic, but on a scale of 1 to 100, she only gave herself a 25—closer to a casual interest then expertise. "Everyone watches his videos," she explained, "The experts are the ones who actually try it. All of it. Not just the everyday looks, but the bold looks." Expertise is not about what they watch, but what they do after they watch.

Learning new skills also has social benefits for this generation, such as finding communities around specific topics. YouTube and Reddit are popular choices for this. While playing video games seems to outsiders like a solitary activity, it is actually one of the most social. Gamers are constantly talking to each other through communication tools like Discord, communicating on Reddit threads, and watching, commenting and interacting with other gamers on YouTube.

In contrast, when Generation Z spends time on entertainment—watching mindless YouTube videos on autoplay, binge-watching "Switched at Birth" or "Umbrella Academy" on their parents' Netflix accounts—they are not left with a warm and fuzzy feeling. Instead, they are left with guilt because they know they could be spending their time better. This is in stark contrast to Millennials who feel more relaxed after unplugging for a few hours… or a few days. Yet another indicator that Generation Z is a generation of doers.

Scheduling Chaos

Generation Z feels overwhelmed by their schedules, and with good reason. They have classes and to-do lists and appointments and extracurriculars and social events and they are all coming from different platforms. They likely have a shared family calendar, and often a personal reminders or to-do list. They also have a class schedule, class (teacher created) to-do lists, and homework assignments on Canvas (or a similar school software). They take notes on what their homework is in class, in documents on their laptop. Many use Evernote and/or the Notes app on their phones for quick memos.

On top of that, friends text info about where/when to meet, they get emailed schedules for extracurriculars, and they find out about other events going on in their school via Snapchat. They might also have group chats on GroupMe (which is slightly more popular with the college crowd than with high school students). On GroupMe, they may have 15+ groups that they follow, maybe one for a group project, one for an organization they belong to, one for the club sports team, one for the fraternity, one for the … you get the idea. Also, if they are doing group projects, they are likely working in Google Drive and also using either the chat functionality or Google Hangouts chat.

Basically, they need a "life raft" to keep track of everything.

One of the most popular ways to track everything is to do a version of calendar blocking for every event and to-do item. Here is an example:

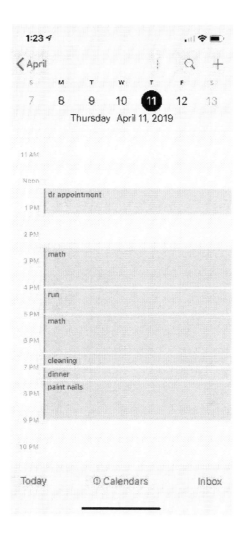

Wow! To be a teen again—I'd love to have an hour and a half to do my nails. But what this is showing is that there is no longer a distinction between to-do items and calendar items. What happens if our day does not go as planned? What happens if an activity runs long? What if we are slightly off-schedule? Do we have to reschedule everything? And what happens when this child becomes that entrepreneur that they were meant to be and they have 10 times the amount of things to do than fit on a schedule. Where do they store the extras?

While this strategy of time-blocking every part of your day (and for every event and to-do list item in the same way) as calendar items may feel like the only option for a time-crunched, stressed out Generation Z, is not a scalable solution. Would some reader out there *please* invent some sort of app to track all of this and put it in one place? Generation Z would love you for it.

Night Owls

In conducting interviews, one thing that alarmed me was how late these teens are staying awake. Generation Z is categorically sleep deprived. Many other studies have replicated these findings, and even shown that sleep deprivation is especially prevalent in females.[51] Modern lifestyles and digital consumption prevent Generation Z from getting adequate sleep, inciting stress and creating new opportunities for brands to offer solutions.

Generation Z stays up late, often until after 11pm and even midnight on school nights, gazing at their phones or their video game consoles. What is most interesting is that when interviewed, they did not perceive their bedtimes as late, and often told us comparative stories of how their other friends stay up even later, playing video games until 3am on school nights. They seemed earnest when we interviewed them, but time is a funny thing, and when you are engrossed in something (like the writing of this book, for example!) it seems to stand still. I wondered if they just were not aware of how much time they were spending at night on their phones, or possibly they did not perceive a bedtime of 11pm or later to be "late." I also wondered if friends were exaggerating how late they routinely stay up because although many told me about stories of friends, I did not interview any teens who admitted to staying up past 1am on a routine basis.

It is recommended that teenagers ages 14-17 should get 8-10 hours of sleep each night, but the average teen gets around 7. About 75 percent of students describe themselves as sleep deprived.[52] One survey of 900 students age 12-15 revealed that 1 in 5 students reports "almost always" waking up during the night.[53] Today's teens require caffeine in the mornings and are sluggish during the day. This suggests that teens may be developing a sleep disorder as a result of late-night scrolling.

What are these teens and young adults doing late at night on their phones? Three main activities take this spot.

Most popular would be watching videos. This takes place mostly on YouTube, often times set to autoplay and a number of teens do report routinely falling asleep to it. Sleep stories on YouTube and on apps like Calm are becoming increasingly popular for this age group as well. These are meditative talking apps to get them to fall asleep. They are also doing more interactive things that are postponing sleep instead of encouraging it.

Second, they are messaging each other via text or iMessage, Snapchat, and Instagram. They are also scrolling, reading, and watching on social media feeds, namely Instagram and Snapchat. It seems that no matter what time of the day, you can always find Generation Z scrolling.

Third, they are playing video games. Gaming has surged in popularity over the past few years, and it is no longer just the boys. 97 percent of teen boys game, and so do 83 percent of teen girls. 92 percent of teen boys and 75 percent have a dedicated gaming console, often in their bedrooms.[54]

Constant Alarms

For most in Generation Z, the primary way to keep track of where and when they have to be seems to be through alarms on their phone. These alarms are constant, and used for virtually anything and everything because it is the only thing that seems to work in their world, even a little.

In one study, I was conducting intercept interviews in a college cafeteria. It was just after lunch and the student's alarm went off to notify him that he had to leave for his class. Suddenly, over the next 5 minutes, a wave of alarms went off, rippling through the cafeteria, dings, rings and vibrations of all sorts. The student we were speaking with did not even notice. This was apparently so common that he had simply tuned it out.

These alarms were both eye-opening and a little funny. They reminded me of class bells that we used to ignore (the old-school version of snooze?). But these diligent Generation Z kids are doing everything they can to be on time. Millennials would wait until that 3rd late bell while trying to compose the perfect excuse in their heads as to why they were late to class, but Gen Z? Gen Z gonna be on time.

Delight In Hacks

Generation Z is obsessed with tracking time, managing time, and optimizing time. It is for this reason that they delight in hacks. They search for the term hacks. They talk about hacks. They use hashtags with the word "hacks" and they have curated lists and boards for hacks.

For Generation Z, hacks are a lifestyle. They are addictive because they speak to a mental model / customer value of time efficiency. However, the modern-day version of hacks has evolved to mean more than just shortcuts. These can equate to cleverness and resourcefulness.

Always reaching behind your desk to fish for your power cord? Fasten a binder clip to the edge and feed the cord through. #Hack

Hacks are no longer just about time.

---

5 TAKEAWAYS FOR MARKETERS

1. **Pair with content Generation Z can feel good about:** Most brands pair their ads with entertainment, but this generation associates entertainment with wasted time, and feels guilt in these moments. Instead, connect your brand to content that is inspiring or educational that this generation will feel good about.

2. **Focus on invisible tech, lighting-fast experiences:** For this generation, time is intrinsically associated with your customer experience. If your interface wastes their time in any way, it's over. They're out. The name of the game here is to make your technology invisible. If they notice your technology, you are doing something wrong. Especially when switching between devices, everything is about speed. Create a lightning-fast experience, or don't bother creating anything at all. Your Generation Z users will not wait for your interface to catch up.

3. **Relieve their schedule chaos:** There is no good way for Generation Z to keep track of all the things they have to do. Anything you can do to simplify their time tracking or to-do list would create a sense of relief. If you are marketing an event, make sure it has an "Add to Calendar" button. For appointments, create automatic email and/or text message reminders. Enable re-scheduling online that they can do themselves 24/7 without having to contact you.

4. **Feature hacks:** Generation Z is obsessed with hacks. Can your marketing content teach people to do something in a clever, resourceful way? Call it a "hack" and add it to your marketing, social media, or content strategy.

5. **Get them to dream sweet dreams of your brand:** Modern lifestyles and constant digital consumption are preventing Generation Z from getting adequate sleep, inciting stress and creating opportunities for brands to provide solutions. If you know your users are watching your videos late at night, know that they might fall asleep to autoplay. Content is the name of the game here: ensure that you have enough videos to enable autoplay for hours. You can even try sponsoring sleep stories or labeling some of your channels as nighttime videos.

MONEY MINDSET: EARNEST AND ENTREPRENEURIAL

Big Money; Big Savers

Generation Z is set to be a massive economic force in coming years. There is big money in this audience; how could there not be when this generation is on track to becoming the largest generation by 2020? Even today, Generation Z makes up 40 percent of U.S. consumers and is set to be the most financially powerful generation in coming years.[55] As teens, Generation Z accounts for $830B per year in the U.S., 7 percent of total consumer spending. The average weekly allowance is $16.90, equating to $44B in direct buying power annually.

Direct purchases are but a measly fraction of their influential spending though. When you include what parents and caregivers spend on Generation Z today, this number skyrockets to $255 billion. Additionally, when you add in total household expenditures, the impact of Generation Z's influence on other household spending may be more than $655 billion.[56]

On top of how much they spend, this generation saves! Generation Z grew up in an era of economic uncertainty and social change, and in contrast to older generations, they are incredibly responsible with their money. This is largely attributed to the environment in which they were raised: they grew up watching their parents struggle financially during a recession and witnessing Millennials coming out of college burdened with mountains of student debt.

As a result, they are ardent savers. In fact, a quarter (25 percent) of this generation say they would rather save for the future than spend money they do not have. Just under that (22 percent) claim they do not spend on "unnecessary, frivolous things". This differs substantially from older generations, where 53 percent of Millennials, 61 percent of Generation X, and 39 percent of Baby Boomers claim they are most likely to spend the majority of what they have on "life in the now".[57]

Generation Z aspires to financial independence and security. In fact, 60 percent of Generation Z (in the U.S. and UK) state that they want to be well off, in stark contrast to only 25 percent of Millennials.[58] They set goals to go into profitable career choices and they are inventing novel ways to earn an income.

Future Earning Potential

Financial stability is a key driver for this group, and they are not waiting until they graduate to start earning. This generation takes action!

Today, the average age of opening a savings account is 13 years old.[59] They probably did not go to a bank to set that up, though, as almost all banking for this age group is done on their mobile device. These kids are saving heavily for college because they have seen Millennials struggle and know that they do not want to be saddled with debt in that way.

Consequently, they are prioritizing the careers and jobs that pay well. At colleges and universities across the country, we are seeing an uptick in students choosing majors in Science, Technology,

Engineering, and Math (STEM). These majors are being studied more than with their Millennial predecessors, the free spirits who followed their passions because they were told they were special. When Generation Z enters college, however, future earning potential is top of mind. They lean toward jobs that will increase their chances at a lucrative future, even if that means setting a passion to the side. 65 percent of Generation Z says it is their goal in life to make it to the top of their profession, compared to 43 percent of Millennials.[60] Innovation consultant Jeremy Finch believes it is more than a decision; it is a compulsion: "They're obsessed with developing contingency plans to help them navigate the dynamic job market."[61]

Generation Z sees the value in traditional education more than their predecessors. While 40 percent of Millennials believed the could have a rewarding career without going to college, only 25 percent of Generation Z felt the same way.[62]

As teenagers, they are even thinking about retirement planning. Were you thinking about retirement when you were 16? I know that I wasn't!

Across the country, this youth audience is even seeking out formal training in financial planning, and many high schools have begun to offer these types of courses as a result of budding interest.[63]

Value For The Money

This generation is earnest, hard-working, and responsible. But this Generation is not what you would call "cheap" either. They will spend money if they believe it is a high value for the dollar amount—up to half their earnings! Listen up, brands: this generation expects more value for their money than previous generations, and they will not stay loyal unless they get that perceived value every time.

Family Influence

Compared to past generations, today's youth are more accepting of their parents' input, especially as it relates to suggestions about money, savings, and how to grow wealth. Knowing that their parents navigated a recession and came out the other end, they trust their experiences and wisdom.

More than that, they actually ask about it. They are interested in learning from others (especially their parents whom they trust implicitly) and soaking in everything they can learn about how to make money and maximize wealth.

Entrepreneurial Mindset

61 percent of Generation Z who are still in high school and 43 percent of Generation Z who are in college say they want to start their own business.[64] There are a number of factors contributing to this shift, but one thing is clear: Generation Z may disrupt the traditional college-to-career pathway.

They idolize YouTube and Instagram creators who get sponsored and paid by brands. This Internet-famous lifestyle was something that a surprisingly large number aspired to be, and some had even gone from thinking to doing and tried it out. Others were too timid to go for it quite yet, but they fantasized and pretended. One 13-year-old played for me hysterical Snapchat videos of she and her friends pretending (just to each other) to be famous YouTubers.

Even if they are not trying to be an influencer themselves, they respect and support others embarking on the endeavor. In speaking about content creators who share video of themselves playing games on YouTube, one 18-year-old gamer said:

I support small businesses, so it's cool to be able to support an individual who's getting their footing in the [gaming] industry. On YouTube, it's hard to get ad revenue. You could branch off and go to Twitch... play games and live stream while people donate money. Or you could do Patrion, where people pledge a certain amount each month from $1 to as high as $50, and you get extra content that's not available to the public. No matter how you do it, it's a career you've made for yourself on YouTube and you're doing it on your own.

Of the entrepreneurs that wind up not becoming paid lifestyle influencers (devastating), one popular choice is to go into social entrepreneurship. Social listening reveals that Generation Z is determined to "make a difference" and "make an impact."[65] But we knew that already: both Millennials and Generation Z are committed to making the world a better place. The difference is that Millennials grew up as optimists, constantly told they were special in their own unique way and deserved a beautiful world. Generation Z, on the other hand, grew up to become realists after being raised in a world filled with consistent reminders of what is wrong and needs to be changed. The combination of this generation's future-focus and work ethic gives me confidence they will be the generation to bring about change that sticks.

Today, more than a third of the workforce chooses self-employment. For 79 percent of those who are self-employed, it is because they make more money that way than by taking a full-time position at a company.[66]

Technology has made it more possible than ever before for teens to land their "side hustle" or (ahem) "part-time job" as we older people used to call it. About a year ago, I interviewed a young lady named Roz. Like many in Generation Z, Roz found herself on YouTube quite often. She was a student at a community college, and she lived within a couple miles of campus in a bright first-floor apartment. It was small, maybe 500 square feet, and very, very beige. Beige walls. Beige carpet. Beige counters. Beige cabinets. She had one framed piece of art on the wall that she said she got from Ikea. It was a portrait of a flower and it brought a cheerful calm to the space. While her living room was small, about a quarter of it was dedicated to a pristine mint-colored vanity set with a matching padded bench (the padding, also beige) and large lighted mirror. It had drawers with ornate bronze pulls to hold Roz's makeup, and an iPad propped up in the back, ostensibly so she could watch YouTube makeup tutorials while trying it out, expressing her art through pallets and mascara.

I asked her about it, and the young entrepreneur explained that she was making money while going to school by doing makeup. Everything she needed to know she learned on YouTube. She was African American and she said that she would not have known how to apply makeup for light complexions without these videos. Because of YouTube, she was able to make enough on the side white going to school to live by herself instead of with a roommate.

Technology is changing the way we work. Generation Z fully understands that they have all the tools at their disposal for them to learn new skills, find jobs, and build businesses to set up a stable financial future for themselves. In Roz's case, it was a fun part-time job that enabled her to have her own place.

As Generation Z entrepreneurs enter the workplace, we are seeing an explosion of trendy co-working spaces. Take WeWork for example, In just 7 short years, WeWork has been able to expand to 218 locations in 53 cities. Generation Z is a large group of self-starters with the tech skills and drive to turn business plans into reality, and businesses are starting up all over the pace to support that. I would expect over the next 10 years to see many more like it, maybe even some created by members of Generation Z themselves.

This generation is taking action—and achieving. Often we see them starting really early, and kids as young as 13 are starting businesses from their parent's kitchen tables are crushing it. I interviewed a 13-year-old who makes upwards of $1k per day (per DAY!) by playing with toys on YouTube. With low startup costs and intuitive tech skills, even young teens are earning an income. What's more, parents are standing behind them, not understanding most of it (I mean... just filming yourself playing with toys?) but nonetheless cheering them on.

This generation is made up of smart, determined hustlers with self-starter tendencies. Rock on with your bad selves, future entrepreneurs. The world needs you!

Think for a moment about the possibilities of recruiting these driven kids for your organization. Imagine the changes they could make as intrapreneurs as well. What an opportunity for the future of our companies.

Network marketing companies have a big opportunity here as well to tap into these budding entrepreneurs. These kids are so tech savvy and creative online—if given the space to really try something new, it is possible that they could sell in ways that these companies really have not even imagined before.

Sweat Now, Glow Later

For Millennials, money seems to be something that "just happens". It is electronic, instant, and easy. They order a ride and it shows up. They order food from their phone and it is delivered to their door. This perception of on-demand ease extends to attitudes toward money as well. Generation Z is very different in this way, as they do not expect money to "just happen." Through exhaustive planning and work, they make it happen.

In stark contrast, Generation Z resembles a much older generation in their traditional views of money and career advancement. While their personal views on race, gender, identity, and sexuality may be liberal, their money mindset is far from it. This generation is hard-working and frugal. They don't mind working a lot if it is going to pan out in the future. On top of that, they religiously save, and they expect more for their money than generations before them.

Many in this generation are in college or just about to start college. With student loans and credit cards available at every turn, they certainly have had ample opportunity to spend. They live by the mantra, "Sweat now, glow later" and rather than indulging, they prefer to save for their future. They will defer purchases rather than going into debt, which is something we do not see with Millennials.

Perception Of Cash, Venmo, and Easy-Pay Options

Cash is as toxic to a Generation Z kid as calling someone by phone. Cash is a thing of the past, and if they have it, this generation does not quite seem to know what to do with it. In fact, they describe it as disposable, for use in for small, unplanned or impulse purchases. One interview participant told us, "Cash is for throw-away stuff like food trucks." Others echoed this sentiment as well.

Financial sharing apps like Venmo have revolutionized the way youth shares and transfers money. Remember when we were young, and splitting checks was a massive headache? You had to remind people in your party to bring singles! Today, splitting checks with a big group of people into a pretty quick process when one person pays and then everyone else Venmos them. Venmo is interesting because it has turned what used to be a bit of a painful process (paying for something or reimbursing someone) into a fun, social experience with pithy comments that your friends can see.

"All the meats" one teen wrote to his friend when he Venmo'd him $15 to pay him back for a burger and fries.

It is a quick and easy tool to lend a hand as well: one participant felt good about helping out a friend in class who had forgotten her wallet and needed cash for a subway card to get home. He gave her a 20 dollar bill, and she immediately Venmo'd him $20 to pay him back.

Yet as helpful as Venmo seems to Generation Z, other ways of making payment simpler like Apple Pay or "Buy it Now" buttons do not have the same appeal. Gen Z describes Apple Pay as feeling less secure. One research participant said, "I don't trust Apple Pay. I like that credit card feel in my hand. It just feels more secure. I mean, what if I lost my phone?" While these are the types of statements participants make, they are not actually worried about security. They said this, but they did not mean it.

Through laddering interviews, it became clear that what these young participants meant by saying this is that using quick tools like Apple Pay or "Buy It Now" buttons felt too easy, and scared them a little because they did not trust themselves to monitor their purchases. Mentally, it did not feel like they were spending money, and that frightened them. There is nothing to sign. Nothing to approve. For a Generation Z youth concerned with saving every penny and maximizing wealth—one who has witnessed older siblings and friends drowning in credit card debt—using easy-pay options feels risky. In fact, this fiscally responsible generation often prefers shopping in-store.

5 TAKEAWAYS FOR MARKETERS

1. **Encourage the hustle:** Generation Z is a cohort of self-starters who place a premium on career advancement and entrepreneurial ventures. Show this audience how your brand or product will help them advance their careers, make money, or save money. Encourage the hustle with Instagram posts, games, and competitions with and brand-aware hashtags.

2. **Focus on outcomes:** This hard-working generation will spend money if they believe the value is high enough. Show them the value in benefits, not in service offerings. What will they ultimately get out of it? Stories and testimonials help.

3. **Tap into entrepreneurs:** They ardently respect entrepreneurs. Showcase stories of entrepreneurs who have used your product or endorse your brand—even your own founder's startup story.

4. **Partner with co-working spaces:** As Generation Z enters the workforce, we are seeing an explosion in co-working spaces because of the sheer number of freelancers, startups, and virtual working. Partner with and advertise in trendy co-working spaces.

5. **Cash is toxic:** Have PayPal and Venmo options easily available, and do not ever make them pay in cash.

BUYING DECISIONS AND BRAND LOYALTY

Generation Z is categorically more financially-responsible than previous generations, with fewer credit cards, less debt, and a preference for saving.[67] In addition, these traditional values extend to a focus on striving for financial stability with career aspirations, as well as greater expectations surrounding getting value for their money.

While their parents are surely delighted, if you are a retailer, you should be feeling the pressure right about now. Predicting spend patterns for this generation has been inconsistent and often discouraging over the years as we marketers were trying to figure these kids out.

However, there is a silver lining. Perk up marketers: you will want to hear this. Generation Z may be is frugal, but they are not cheap. In fact, when they feel that something is worth the money, they are willing to spend over half of their monthly earnings for it!

In this section, we will talk about some of the intricacies related to how a Generation Z consumer makes a purchase decision.

Exhaustive Research

For Generation Z, what influences purchases more than price is the ultimate value that they will get for their money. Big purchases especially are exhaustively researched, compared, and personal reviews read.

When Millennials are making a big purchase, they read reviews too, but not nearly as many. When researching products on a website like Amazon, Millennials will look at the star ratings and hone in on the 5-star ratings and the 1-star ratings. They will likely skip reading reviews for anything in between.

In contrast, for a large purchase, Generation Z will read every review, no matter what the rating. They will take the time to do this and carefully weigh the value they are getting for their money. Not only that, they will look up what people are saying about the product outside of the website or app where they are buying it. For instance, I was in an interview while a young woman in her early 20s was buying a pair of sneakers. She had seen them on Instagram originally and then bounced between websites to find the best price and to read all the reviews she could find. She ultimately purchased them through the retailer's website, but before she did, she spent a great deal of time on Instagram and then on Pinterest pouring through ideas of how to style the shoes, what to wear with them, and getting ideas for the value that she would get from these shoes. She paid attention not just to the fashion, but also what people were doing in the photos. She noted how they looked and made assumptions about their lifestyle, what they liked to do, and similarities between her and the imagined lives of people in photos on Instagram.

The Coupon Craze Ends With Millennials

Millennials are coupon crazy.[68] Finding coupons are an important part of the research phase. The moment they see a "Promo Code" box on a checkout page, Millennials will stop their purchase to go look for a coupon code. They have multiple coupon apps on their phones, and browsing through Groupons can be a part of their daily routines. Many get daily emails and push notifications from the apps.

Coupons for Millennials feel irresistible, driving behavior, and add a sense of urgency to the purchase. If they miss a coupon, they feel so upset, like they have lost money—even if it was not something they were planning to purchase to begin with.

However, Generation Z is not like this. In fact, Generation Z is 2-3 times more likely to be influenced by a brand's engagement on social media than by sales or discounts, making them the only generation to value social media over price when it comes to making purchase decisions.[69]

Research And Buy Behaviors

By no means does this indicate that Generation Z is less price sensitive. On the contrary, Generation Z does extensive research before buying most products, and for easy-to-find products, is certainly influenced by lower prices. Before buying anything, this generation watches multiple YouTube videos, scans product reviews, checks Reddit (for some items), and more. Despite an 8-second attention span, Generation Z shoppers view 62 percent more pages during a browsing session than other demographics, and bounce 51 percent less of the time.[70].

In terms of buying decisions, low prices are only part of the picture. While 26 percent of Generation Z choose a retailer because of lower pricing, 23 percent base their buying decisions on the user experience: how easy it is to find products and use your website or mobile app. In fact, 60 percent of Generation Z will not use an app or website that is too slow to load; 62 percent will not use an app if it is difficult to navigate.[71]

This means that just as important as your price is the ease of your buying experience.

In Generation Z, we are seeing a slight uptick in the percentage who shop in brick-and-mortar stores. This may change as they enter the workforce and have less free time, but for now, 79 percent say that both online and physical stores offer the brands they want, and 70 percent believe they can find lower pricing in stores.[72] When online retailers get the order, it is because the experience is superb (products feel easier to find), or because there is a larger selection (more choices) available for unique and independent Generation Z.

While Millennials are arguably just as tech-savvy as their younger counterparts, Generation Z increasingly uses technology as a purchase platform and a method for engaging in brand conversations. 85 percent, in fact, learn about new products on social media, and 29 percent of "older" Generation Z members list social media as the most influential method to gain awareness of a brand.

Combine that with the fact that Generation Z is twice as likely to convert on mobile as any other generation, and you can see how important it is to continue brand engagement on social media, even if some of your messages may get lost in the noise.[73]

Retailers have already begun to reach out to the generation in new, interactive ways that leverage a dynamic combination of social media, video, and live feeds. For instance, Bloomingdale's and Cotton Inc. rolled out an interactive 60-second, live video fashion show where viewers could click through to browse and buy featured outfits and share directly on social media. The interactive video with 80 items to choose from went up on fashion site *Who What Wear* and was streamed on social media.[74] It is these creative fresh-format interactions that brands will need to continue in the future if they wish to stay relevant with this generation.

Sharing Purchases

Generation Z eagerly share *potential* purchases with friends via social media, but not *actual* purchases. In their minds, once they have purchased something, it feels like bragging to tell people about it.

That's right: they feel bad sharing that they got a good deal. This is such a foreign concept to Millennials: telling everyone how they got a deal seems to particularly joyful.

The most interesting part about this finding is that when we consider the customer's journey, many of companies focus on post-purchase as the phase to encourage customers to share their purchases with friends. For Generation Z customers, to be most effective, this effort would need to take place earlier in the journey: somewhere in the research stage.

Want The True Cost

Because Generation Z started shopping online at such an early age, even by the time they were teenagers, they were keenly aware of what it feels like to have been burned by unexpected shipping costs or special taxes and fees on a phone plan or plane ticket. Consequently, Generation Z wants the "out-the-door" price.

What does this mean for you? For this audience, make your price all-inclusive, show them the value, and then do not try to upcharge them. This generation loves all-inclusive travel destinations so that there are no financial surprises.

Now, this should be a no-brainer to you, but shipping costs are totally unacceptable and complete deal breakers for this Generation (yes, Amazon changed everything). When shopping online, Generation Z actually prefers to go direct to the retailer's website instead of an aggregator like Amazon. For instance, as long as the price is equivalent, they will buy shoes directly through Nike.com. But the moment there is a line item that says "shipping", the experience is broken, and a bad taste is left in their mouth. They may pay the shipping if they really want the product, but the damage is done and they will be less likely to shop with you again.

Midweek Impulse Purchases

For older Generation Z (and young Millennials who live alone), it seems that they are more susceptible to impulse buying midweek. This is mostly due to the fact that they are alone. During the week, these young, energetic Generation Z's work, commute, maybe go to the gym, but that is about it. They do not hang with their friends or significant other until the weekend. 53 percent visit stores in-person during the week, and even more sit at home on their phones, browsing and buying.[75]

Experiences Versus Things

What's more valuable: experiences or things? The answer may surprise you. For years, studies have shown us that Millennials value experiences more highly than physical things. Even our Millennial studies have shown us that the experiences that Millennials choose to spend money on (e.g., trips, concerts, art pop-ups) are considered necessary to recharge from everyday pressures. Millennials tend to work a number of small odd jobs to pay for them. Maybe they drive Lyft or Uber on the side, or take market research studies. Either way, 78 percent of Millennials say they would choose to spend money on an experience rather than buying something desirable.[76]

However, this is not necessarily the same for Generation Z. In contrast, Generation Z values products you can touch and hold, with 60 percent saying they would prefer a cool product over a cool experience.

Given that Millennials prefer the experience and Generation Z prefers the product, how does a company position themselves differently for these two unique audiences?

Take the example of a gaming company. For Millennials who prioritize experiences, this company should focus its marketing efforts on showing the experience of gaming, the feeling users get when they share with friends, on forums and in the conversation. Generation Z, on the other hand, cares more about value exchange. In this case, gamers might even be satisfied with intangibles, such as in-game unlockables (e.g., maps, trophies, skins for characters, new tanks). When Amazon began to partner with Blizzard Entertainment to sell its games, Blizzard decided to offer free in-game loot to Amazon Prime subscribers. This value exchange gave young, product-focused gamers yet another reason to stay subscribed to Amazon's premium service and turned out to be highly successful at retaining young customers as Prime members.[77]

The message here: Same company, two strategies for positioning, informed by broad generational preferences.

Parent-Teen Shopping Experiences

Today's teens are master negotiators, manipulating—er, promising their parents things like better grades or additional chores to get them to buy things for them when they are in stores together, sometimes even offering to pay for a portion of the purchase themselves.[78] In fact, when shopping with their teen children, mothers may spend up to 30 percent more than they would have without them, and 42 percent of parents of Generation Z children admit to buckling under their child's emotional pleas and purchase pressure.[79] Fromm and Read refer to this communication pattern as the "pester power" of kids and teens, and I like that term!

As a parent myself, I expected that. But what I did not expect was that the influence pattern runs both ways; teens are just as likely to be influenced by their parents when they are making purchases. Compared to past generations, today's youth are more accepting of their parents' input, especially as it relates to suggestions about money, savings, and how to grow wealth.

Brand Loyalty

When working with brands to understand their customers better, we are frequently asked to find out more about loyalty: what would turn first-time or return buyers into repeat customers? So let's talk about what we make of this generation's brand loyalty and what kind of loyalty programs will and will not resonate for this demographic.

If you have reached this point in the book, you know by now that this generation is hard-working, entrepreneurial, and financially responsible. With these traits come increased expectations: Generation Z expects more value for their money than previous generations, and they will not remain loyal unless they feel that value—every time. Quick and easy online shopping is also to blame for diminished loyalty: for Generation Z, who grew up researching products and services on their phones, it takes a matter of seconds to find alternatives. This presents quite a challenge for name brands striving to grow loyalty with this group.

Generation Z is frugal, but they will pay more for a better product. Consequently, they are less likely to be moved by either coupons or traditional loyalty programs.[80] In fact, over half of 18 to 21-year-olds said they like to experiment with different brands, even when they know there is one that works well for them. Conversely, only 33 percent of Generation X and 25 percent of Baby Boomers would switch to a new brand if they knew there was one they liked.[81]

When choosing between name brands and private label brands (i.e., store brands), 60 percent of Generation Z does not have a preference right off the bat. Over 80 percent indicate price is the most critical factor when making a purchase though, and 50 percent believe name brands are "much more expensive" than private label brands.[82] Of the Generation Z consumers who do purchase name brands regularly, they do this for two key reasons. The first is because they want an assurance of the product's quality, not because they feel a connection to the brand. The second (and more important reason) is because a friend, family member, or online personality (e.g., Instagram or YouTube influencer) referred them to the brand.

Even if they choose not to repeat a purchase, 68 percent would still refer a name brand to a friend if they believed in the product. But that might not be saying much, as 41 percent said they would be willing to refer any product for an incentive.[83]

Though Generation Z is not generally brand loyal, when they do commit to a brand, it is for these key reasons:

1. Superior customer experience

2. Brand aligns with the consumer's personal values

3. Speed: faster checkout and delivery

4. Family or friend recommendation

The top reason that Generation Z is more likely to be loyal is because of a frictionless customer experience that includes an excellent mobile interface, top-notch customer service, and speed. For Generation Z, their phone is basically just an extension of their body. No matter where they are, they demand a frictionless experience with no lag time from switching between devices (say, jumping from a laptop to a phone to in-store). They use their smartphones everywhere, especially while shopping in-store, and far more than any other generation of consumer.

Generation Z is flowing between devices in with unprecedented fluidity and requires flawless interconnection in the user interfaces and customer experiences to enable them to continue their mental flow, even after switching from laptop to phone to tablet and back again. Many in Generation Z also have smart speakers such as Amazon Echo or Google Home, and smart devices including wearables, smart toys, and drones. By 2020, it is forecasted that 8.4 billion connected things will be in use worldwide, and eventually Generation Z will live in a world with 1 trillion interconnected devices! These devices, not yet imagined, will re-shape how this generation lives, works, and plays. Lightning-fast, uninterrupted transitions and cloud storage are essential for Generation Z's uber-connected world.[84]

Spotify is a prime example of a brand that garners incredible loyalty among its young customers. According to a survey done by Venture Capital firm Goldwater Capital, 92 percent of Spotify subscribers plan to either keep their existing service or upgrade. This is, in large part, because of its mobile user experience and personalization. While Spotify offers essentially the same service as Apple Music and Amazon Music, Generation Z subscribers are head-over-heels obsessed with the brand. Goldwater called it "undisputed customer love" it its report. In fact, among shoppers under 30 (an age range which represents the core target market for tune streaming services and products) Spotify's Net Promoter Score (NPS) ranking was a 32. The next highest NPS ranking was Apple Music at 15.[85]

For Generation Z, brand loyalty may also be associated with personal values. For example, if young consumers feel that the brand understands them as an individual (53 percent) or has a socially-responsible brand message they agree with (56 percent), they seek out more brand interaction.[86]

The third reason boils down to speed. One study cited the following reasons for Generation Z's repeat purchases. You will notice that in most of these, an integration with new tech is what results in faster checkout and delivery:[87]

- Same-day delivery
- One-hour delivery made by drone
- Mobile self-checkout at a brick-and-mortar store
- Voice checkout with a smart speaker (e.g., Amazon Echo, Google Home, Google Assistant, Siri)
- Wearable checkout (e.g., buying from a watch)
- Checkout through social media or chat apps

Offering same-day delivery and mobile self-checkouts in brick-and-mortar stores may be key to boosting loyalty for this generation. This makes sense as a large portion of this generation not only shops in physical stores, but also use their smartphones while in-store.

Finally, while not unique to Generation Z, we do still find loyalty from customer recommendations: friends and family who recommended the product or brand.

For this generation, it seems that a better user experience, feel-good branding, sheer speed, and family/friend recommendations may trump any form of a traditional loyalty program.

Convenience And Time Savings

For Generation Z, everything is about convenience and time savings. While older generations are concerned about anonymity online, Generation Z is comfortable sharing personal data in exchange for a more personalized experience. Millennials and Gen Z are over 25 percent more likely than Gen X and Baby Boomers to opt for a predictive Internet. The study goes farther finding 50 percent of Gen Z would stop visiting a website if it didn't anticipate what they needed, liked or wanted. This predictability relies on the fact that users need a seamless experience.

One example can be found in eating. An average Generation Z gets takeout three to four times a week, usually using mobile delivery apps. Convenience is a major reason for Gen Z's takeout habit, whether they are using a delivery app or picking it up themselves. They do not mind paying extra for that convenience either. An International Foodservice Manufacturers Association (IFMA) survey found that Gen Zers are willing to pay more than older generations for food delivery: 54 percent said they would pay $3 to $5, and 19 percent said they would pay $6 to $10.[88]

Craig Key, Chief Marketing Officer of Minneapolis-based food delivery app Bite Squad, claims Generation Z is one of the company's largest audience groups: "Where they spend and how they spend is based on experiences, and they spend on convenience. So, a service like ours, or Lyft, a ride-sharing service, or other digital marketplaces that connect buyers and sellers and create conveniences are going to do really well with that audience."[89]

5 TAKEAWAYS FOR MARKETERS

1. **Support the research phase:** Help Generation Z along in their exhaustive research. Give them scannable details they need in a quick visual—for instance, a matrix of all the services or features you offer and how you stack up against competitors.

2. **Sharing takes place pre-purchase:** To encourage Generation Z to share purchases, remind them during the research stage instead of post-purchase where most brands tend to focus.

3. **Experiment with new ways to capture loyalty:** Brand loyalty is harder than ever to earn. Do not waste your time with coupons (thank goodness!) The following elements trump traditional loyalty programs for Generation Z: (1) superior mobile experiences; (2) feel-good branding; (3) sheer speed of checkout and delivery; (4) family/friend recommendations. Focus on enhancing one or all of these for a shot at capturing some elusive Gen Z loyalty.

4. **Give the total total:** Be up front about the total cost of your product. Don't charge extra for the shipping. All-inclusive is best.

5. **Make it easy to buy, and make sure they are aware of their purchase:** Create completely seamless experiences between touchpoints, but add a little friction at checkout: just one extra click makes Generation Z feel better about making an informed purchase decision.

THE FUTURE OF POLITICS AND SOCIAL CHANGE

Research has shown us for some time that both Millennials and Generation Z truly want to make an impact on the world. Generation Z, with its sheer size and empathetic attitudes toward social change, has the potential to drastically change modern politics in the United States. However, the increasing divisiveness of party lines does not align with the mental model and value system held by Generation Z. As a result, political parties will have to shift their positioning in order to capture voters in the very near future, reflecting a more moderate balance of fiscally conservative politics and socially liberal ones.

Not surprisingly, when it comes to views on today's political climate, Millennials and Generation Z have consistently held more socially liberal views than older generations.[90] When we consider modern politics in the United States across a range of issues including immigration, racial equality, climate change, the role of government in our society, the views of Generation Z tend to mirror those of Millennials.[91]

However, what is surprising is the balance of liberal and conservative values we are seeing in Generation Z. "Growing up in an uncertain economy and being raised by more frugal and skeptical Gen X'ers has shaped a less entitled, more money-conscious generational cohort," says Christine Hassler, author of the *20 Something Manifesto.*[92]

As a result, we are seeing a more fiscally responsible group who expects more value for their money. This group worries about savings, for themselves personally as well as for their country. 25 percent of Generation Z say they would rather save for the future than spend money that they do not have. 22 percent say they never spend on "unnecessary, frivolous things". This is in stark contrast to other generations, where 39 percent of Baby Boomers, 61 percent of Generation X, and 53 percent of Millennials claim they are most likely to spend what they have on "life in the now".[93]

When we talk about politics in the United States, we as a society tend to bucket individuals into either liberal or conservative groups. Generation Z is different because they embody values from both of these camps. In comparing survey research to behavioral, qualitative interviews, it's no wonder that people have a hard time figuring out this generation's politics.

A Forbes article has labeled Generation Z the, "Fiscally responsible, tattoo hating, Republican leaning group, touted by conservatives as their best hope for the future, and as the antithesis of Millennials."[94] On likert scales, it is true that Generation Z more often label themselves "conservative" or "moderate", especially when they are comparing themselves to Millennials, a generation they perceive as impulsive and drama-seeking. However, these self-reports are misleading because as humans we often say one thing but do another. As a result, deep qualitative studies make a difference in helping us to more effectively understand the behavioral shifts going on in teens and young adults today.

While Generation Z tends to lean conservative on fiscal issues, they lean left on topics related to social issues. On social topics, they more closely mirror Millennials' attitudes, though admittedly, Millennials continue (at least for now) to remain louder on social change fronts. Nonetheless, these two groups agree on a number of liberal viewpoints related to race, gender, identity and sexuality. For instance, when it comes to race, both Millennials and Generation Z tend to feel that blacks are treated less fairly than whites in the United States, and they are more likely to approve of NFL players kneeling in protest during the national anthem. Most believe that increasing racial and ethnic diversity in the United States is a positive trend in our society, and they are more accepting of interracial and same-sex marriages than preceding generations.

Generation Z also has a never-before-seen global perspective. Just turn on an Xbox One and snap on a headset to communicate with gamers halfway around the world. This boundaryless generation is more global in their thinking, interactions, and empathetic responses. 58 percent of adults worldwide ages 35 and over agree that, "kids today have more in common with their global peers than they do with adults in their own country." This means that an 8-year-old in the U.S. is likely to have more in common with an 8-year-old in India than a 65-year-old in their own country.[95]

It is too soon to draw a conclusion about how the views of this young generation will evolve. Most have yet to reach voting age, and their outlook is still developing through controversial, current issues we have seen happening in the Trump administration. These kids are at a time in their lives where they are starting to pay attention to headlines in a more focused way. What happens in the news over the next couple of years with any number of large-scale discussions in this country are going to prove to be defining moments in the development of political attitudes, beliefs, and values of this generation for years to come.

Based on my own interviews and research with teens, similar to many other generations of teens before them, they are not focused on traditional news. Most of them bump into stories while scrolling through feeds. They wind up reading shared articles, then following the rabbit hole down a path to learn more, if they are interested. Most teens do not have a standard routine when it comes to checking news on a daily basis.

That said, even though they may not follow headlines religiously, they do have opinions about specific "news" topics that they have at least casually researched and discussed with their friends. Some of these include gun control, gun violence in schools, terrorism; student debt; border security; travel bans; racism; LGBTQ issues; equal pay; climate change; drones; surveillance; cryptocurrency; violence in video games; unemployment; homelessness; welfare; depression; mental health; bullying; obesity; sexual activity; abortion; drug use; and marijuana legalization.

You may notice that most of the topics teens are interested in are influenced by personal exposure more so than Internet research. And that makes sense. For example, it's only natural for kids to be worried about guns and gun violence, as they have to participate in terrifying drills and learn to plan for emergencies in the case of a gun-wielding classmate.

In terms of formats for getting news, Generation Z tends to rely on snackable, highly curated, easy-to-read tidbits from aggregation tools like the Skimm or Snapchat. Some rely on Facebook for news (even though they don't use it regularly) because they know that older people spend time there and so the "news feed" seems more authoritative. A Generation Z news consumer is more than likely a visual bumper, someone who relies on feeds on Facebook, Snapchat, or Instagram to stumble into stories of interest.

This is how Aubrey, a 20-year-old college student, told us she kept up with the day's headlines:

> *When I am looking for the news I'll go on Facebook just to see, you know, what news is relevant to me because that would pop up first [scrolling] I am not seeing much of any news on here. So Facebook doesn't always show me something…*

After perusing Facebook, she turned to Instagram:

> *The Shade Room or Baller Alert [on Instagram] typically post big headline news stories that relate to all types of things. Today I do see something relevant to me, something that caught my attention on The Shade Room, [a] repost [from] another news channel place [stops on a story about a bridge collapse near her] and it does impact me because of the occasion and because I have friends… where this incident happened. And it is really upsetting.*

She went on to tell us about news aggregators she has seen:

> *I know there's a News app or something [from] Apple but I don't even have it downloaded. I know I used to, but I don't really look at it often. If a friend tells me something about the news or I got a phone call from someone, I may Google it but typically reading through when it pops on Facebook or Instagram.*

While randomly stumbling into stories on social media may not seem to older generations as the most credible way to get news, the fact that this generation is showing an interest in these topics is a positive sign for our society. It also makes sense given the other behavioral and attitudinal attributes of this generation that as they shift into adulthood, they will become more deeply invested in these issues.

While Millennials were rocking out to cassettes and humming along to the sound of dial-up Internet growing up, Generation Z was raised to feel less safe, frightened about online predators, haunted by terrorist threats, and constantly reminded about the epidemic of school shootings with terrifying videos of kids running out of school buildings reflecting onto their faces from their phones.

Like Millennials before them, Generation Z possesses a genuine desire to make an impact on society. What's more, the other attributes this generation has in large numbers—hard work, diligence, perseverance—are exactly what, as a generation, Millennials have been missing. Generation Z is a cohort of hard-working doers. When it comes to social change, then, Generation Z is ready to stop talking and start implementing.

With nicknames like "philanthro-teens[96]", this generation is bringing about change with modern tools: GoFundMe and social campaigns. High school service hours are not perceived by this group as a requirement; but rather an expected norm.

Generation Z also recognizes the role social media plays in modern news consumption. These teens and young adults are much less likely than older generations to say that getting news from social media is detrimental to society – 39 percent of Gen Zers hold this view, compared with about half of that among each of Millennials, Generation X and Baby Boomers.[97]

While Generation Z's views on modern day politics are still developing, we are seeing trends that provide some compelling clues about where they may be headed and how their views will impact our nation's political landscape.

5 TAKEAWAYS FOR MARKETERS

1. **Do your research:** Research your specific Generation Z customers so that you understand what causes they do and do not care about.

2. **Choose a cause:** Choose a cause related to your brand, and make sure Generation Z knows what your brand stands for. This does not have to be political.

3. **Add social impact to content strategy:** Associate your brand with social impact stories. Share stories that your consumers will be interested in.

4. **Be mindful of isolating customers:** Because of the duality of political beliefs that Generation Z embodies, it would be risky to support a candidate or polarizing issue like free college tuition. Generation Z is fiscally conservative and socially liberal. Any one-sided choice for your brand will isolate large chunks of this audience.

5. **For politicians and political companies:** Our current parties in the U.S. are too divisive for Generation Z. To tap into the potential of this future generation of voters, political candidates and politicians will need to be able to meet in the middle.

THE LONELY GENERATION

Describing a 13-year-old from her research study, a journalist from the Atlantic wrote: "She spent much of her summer keeping up with friends, but nearly all of it was over text or Snapchat. 'I've been on my phone more than I've been with actual people,' she said. 'My bed has, like, an imprint of my body.'"[98]

Today, Generation Z reports higher levels of loneliness and social isolation than 72 year olds. We know they are "connected" but they seem to be disconnected when it comes to each other. Many believe this is a result of social media usage, but a 2018 Cigna survey shows that the two are not correlated. Heavy users of social media had a loneliness similar to those who never use social media.[99]

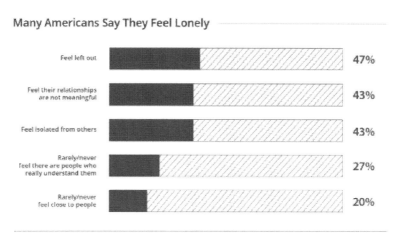

Many Americans Say They Feel Lonely

Feel left out	47%
Feel their relationships are not meaningful	43%
Feel isolated from others	43%
Rarely/never feel there are people who really understand them	27%
Rarely/never feel close to people	20%

Source: 2018 Cigna online survey of 20,096 Americans

This study of more than 20,000 U.S. adults revealed that just under half of Americans feel alone or left out, and almost a third feel that there are rarely or never people who understand them. These stats are troubling, especially when we are talking about today's children and young adults who are supposed to be growing up and having fun.

This generation is nearly twice as likely than Millennials and Generation X to report their mental health as fair or poor. They are also more likely to report having received treatment or therapy from a mental health professional.[100] Being glued to their phones has not just affected mental health; physical health is a real issue as well. This generation has been praised in many ways during their brief time on this earth—motivated entrepreneurs, social advocates—but they also share a less laudable distinction: the first generation to have a shorter life expectancy than their parents due to unprecedented childhood obesity.[101]

This generation is certainly interacting with each other, but through the lens of technology instead of face-to-face. As early as 8 years old, kids are donning headsets and plopping themselves in front of gaming consoles.

As humans, we all crave connection. Generation Z is just finding it in new ways: teen boys in our studies tended to have raw conversations while playing video games; it was the only time they felt they could be real with each other. Perhaps this is one of the reasons gaming has skyrocketed among Generation Z, with 66 percent of teens and young adults listing gaming as their primary hobby (and 45 percent of those female, FYI). Amazon spent $970 million on the acquisition of Twitch, the live streaming video platform where viewers watch playthroughs of video games and other gaming-related events, signifying the expected growth in the marketplace and importance of gaming among Generation Z.[102] The International Olympic

Committee is even considering adding pro-gaming as an official sport in 2024.

The number of teens who get together with friends on a daily basis dropped by more than 40 percent from 2000 to 2015. An article in the Atlantic notes, "It's not only a matter of fewer kids partying; fewer kids are spending time simply hanging out. That's something most teens used to do: nerds and jocks, poor kids and rich kids, C students and A students. The roller rink, the basketball court, the town pool, the local necking spot—they've all been replaced by virtual spaces accessed through apps and the web."[103]

Today's teens are less likely to leave the house without their parents. The shift is stunning: high school seniors in 2015 went out less often than 8th graders in 2009.[104] Driving, once a symbol of adolescent freedom, has even lost its appeal. For Generation X and Baby Boomers, nearly all students had their driver's license by the spring of senior year. Today, more than 1 in 4 teens today still lack one by the end of high school. Moreover, the teens that have a license describe it as something they were pressured by their parents to do.

This generation is less likely to date. Even the vocabulary around dating has shifted. The initial stage of courtship used to be marked by vocabulary about how someone "likes" you. Today, teens call this "talking" instead—an ironic choice for a generation who prefers their thumbs. After two teens have "talked" for a while, they might start dating. But only 56 percent of high school seniors go out on dates; down from 85 percent for Generation X and Baby Boomers.

This decline in dating tracks with a drop in sexual activity and teen pregnancy, and while many see this as a surge of "responsible" behavior among youth, to the researcher looking at all the data as a whole, it is actually quite troubling. It is not rocket science that people who engage in frequent, meaningful in-person interactions feel less isolated and report better health than those who rarely interact face-to-face. One study found that, "Loneliness has the same impact on mortality as smoking 15 cigarettes a day, making it even more dangerous than obesity."[105]

Humans are social creatures, and it is important for the future health of this generation that in-person communities are not replaced by social media. Teens do report being engaged and having fun at in-person events—and why wouldn't they? Humans of all ages need in-person interaction to stay in good mental health.

In past generations, students had communities outside of school: neighbors, extended families, work friends, and church communities. Remember playing with the neighborhood kids? Well, Generation Z most likely does not. Less than 1 in 5 kids today spend time with neighbors several times a week. In 1974, this was 1 in 3. Families are also becoming smaller, and children raised by a single parent has doubled from 15 percent to 31 percent in just 2 decades. Church communities are rapidly dwindling as well. Monthly church attendance has dropped by over 20 percent since 1970. We are also spending less time with friends from work. This has dropped from 2.5 hours a week in the mid-70s to under 1 hour today.[106] Imagine a student being unhappy at school and having no other community to turn to. For many, that is a reality.

As marketers, we have a responsibility to look at the cultural and social trends. If we find that what we do for the benefit of capitalism is having a negative affect on society, we need to be ready to pivot from our course and try something more socially-responsible. This set of takeaways is for the marketer who wants to truly engage and connect; not simply grow in terms of likes and followers.

5 TAKEAWAYS FOR MARKETERS

1. **Stop the superficiality:** As marketers keep blasting noise on social media, today's youth are growing weary of the surface-level noise and crave real connection. Generation Z prioritizes honest, transparent, authentic messages from friends, leaders, employers, and your brand. Provide quality content that inspires, educates, and connects people within your brand community.

2. **Event marketing (in person!):** Forget the online-only conference. Generation Z is seeking in-person social connection. For B2B, in-person events like networking breakfasts, conferences, and trade shows have always been popular, but in this climate of decreasing in-person experiences, it is all the more critical to make your brand stand out. Go to these events with the goal of making genuine connections. For B2C, these events could be anything from fashion shows to social activism based on the goals of your campaigns and the interests of your consumers.

3. **Set up digital communities with in-person events:** Invest in creating communities for your customers who share specific interests related to your brand, or who are interested in learning a particular skill. This will not only build brand engagement, but also help to connect these teens with a tribe, as they are not getting as much social connection elsewhere in their lives. Add

in-person events to digital communities to maximize your impact.

4. **Tap into gaming:** Over 60 percent of teens today rate gaming as their top hobby. Many (males especially) say that this is where they have their most meaningful conversations and feel most connected, regardless of what is blowing up on the console's screen. There are a multitude of communities online for gaming. If your brand could join with one of these communities in a meaningful way that connects well with your brand, you would not only gain a new audience in gamers but also connect more teens and young adults with each other to provide them a community. This could mean a partnership with a community, or it could mean gamifying a piece of your process or website in order to become a part of the conversation.

5. **Highlight your people.** Generation Z is seeking deeper connections all around, and one of the biggest draws of your brand just might be the people they get to interact with.

LEARNING: WHAT EDUCATORS NEED TO KNOW

My research on Generation Z has traditionally been for large companies and organizations: brands who want to know how to be confident in what their specific customers need in order to identify and make bold decisions about going after new market opportunities, launching the right products or services, or optimizing their existing on-screen user experiences.

It came as a surprise, then, when I started getting requests to keynote education conferences. I also started booking research projects with state school boards and other organizations dedicated to improving not only classroom teaching effectiveness, but also our educational systems in the United States and programs that support them. Although I had not planned to have a section in this book for educators, in looking at what the market was telling me, I thought I better add one!

Consequently, this section will have fewer takeaways for the marketer, and more takeaways for the educator. Some of the content I discuss in this section might be slightly repetitive as it has been culled from other sections of this book. My goal with this learning segment was to frame it for educators: to provide a peek at some of the critical takeaways that they should be thinking about for their customers: Generation Z students.

Dear Educators: You are amazing. You affect so many lives. I feel like an amateur compared to those of you who are in the classroom every day with your Generation Z students, the Jane Goodalls of teenagers, learning their strange sounds and body language and (yes) their smells. Nonetheless, I have been honored by the invites to speak at your events and to help you hone your teaching styles and educational programs not just to educate but to inspire—to get them to put down their phones and really pay attention to you in the first place! You are surely more aware than anyone that this generation's habits are new and different. It would not surprise me if you already knew everything in this section. But my hope is to clearly articulate it, so even if you are familiar with it all, we are at least all working with the same vocabulary so we can continue the dialogue to build strategies based on the research, ones that consistently work with this new breed of youth.

It's a brave new world. Let's do this together!

Intellect Is The New Black

When Generation X was growing up, bullying and teasing of the smart kids was a common pastime. Movies like "Clueless" (1995) taught Millennials that being a blonde bimbo was the ideal to live up to: "Do you prefer 'fashion victim' or 'ensembly challenged'?"

It is incredibly refreshing, then, to learn that Generation Z embodies neither of these attitudes. In 2004, just before the oldest in Generation Z started middle school, the overnight pop-culture phenomenon "Mean Girls" came out. This satirical comedy where—spoiler alert—the alpha mean girl winds up getting run over by a bus, seemed to mark the turning point between these two generations.

Generation Z wears their smarts like a badge of honor. They pride themselves on their intelligence, analytical abilities, diligence, and creative problem solving. They enjoy showing off their unique talents: their personal niche in a brand-conscious world.

This group loves learning, and it certainly does not stop when they leave the classroom. They are spending hours every night watching videos and consuming content in order to learn new skills. They are also spending an enormous amount of time seeking inspiration, a craving that creates a glaring opportunity for educators to jump in and fill. 89 percent spend their free time after school engaged in productive activities, instead of just "hanging out". It has been common to lay blame on parents for over-scheduling their teens, but it seems to have made for a more focused, driven generational cohort dedicated to not just talking about their goals, but truly making them happen.

To Generation Z's love of learning, I say: "You go, Glen Coco!"

Money Worries And Career Aspirations

Because this generation grew up in the Great Recession and witnessed their families' struggles, financial stability is a key driver for them. They understand the importance of being prepared for an uncertain financial future and are prioritizing it from a young age. They are not waiting until they graduate high school or college to begin making money. This generation takes action!

Today, the average age for opening a savings account is 13 years old.[107] These kids most likely did not go to a bank to set that up, though, as almost all banking for this age group is done on a mobile device. Teenagers are saving heavily for college from an early age because of what they witnessed Millennials going through: a 92 percent increase in student loan borrowers and a 74 percent increase in average student debt between 2004 and 2014.[108] Generation Z has watched Millennials emerge from universities saddled with debt and they are resolute that they will not end up like this. In fact, 1 in 5 say "debt should be avoided at all costs."[109]

As a result, they are choosing careers that pay well. At colleges and universities across the country, we are seeing an uptick in students choosing majors in Science, Technology, Engineering, and Math (STEM). Millennials were taught that they were special snowflakes who should follow their dreams and live their most authentic lives. When Generation Z enters college, though, future earning potential is top of mind. They lean toward jobs that will increase their chances of a lucrative future, even if that means setting a passion to the side. 65 percent of Generation Z says it is their goal in life to make it to the top of their profession, compared to 43 percent of Millennials.[110] Innovation consultant Jeremy Finch believes it is more than a decision; it is a compulsion: "They're obsessed with developing contingency plans to help them navigate the dynamic job market."[111]

Generation Z sees the value in traditional education more than their predecessors. While 40 percent of Millennials believed they could have a rewarding career without going to college, only 25 percent of Generation Z feel the same way.[112]

As teenagers, they are even thinking about retirement planning. Were you thinking about retirement when you were 16 years old? I know I wasn't!

Across the country, this youth audience is even seeking out formal training in financial planning, and many high schools have begun to offer these types of courses as a result.[113]

Entrepreneurial Drive

Generation Z is driven to pave their own way. In fact, according to one study, 61 percent of high school students and 43 percent of college students would rather be entrepreneurs than employees after graduating from college.[114]

Just over half of high schoolers report that their parents pressure them to gain professional experience while in high school, but just as many also said that their parents have *not* helped them gain this experience. This parenting style (offering advice but not doing it for them) has taught this generation to be independent go-getters when it comes to making money. It has encouraged them to use their own knowledge and creativity to forge new paths to financial success.

This creativity is palpable, as 1 in 4 students in 5th to 12th grade is learning how to start or run a business.[115]

Nearly 1 in 10 already owns a business![116]

On top of that, nearly 1 in 3 want to invent something that changes the world.[117] I don't know about you, but this combination of entrepreneurship and social drive makes me feel pretty optimistic about our future.

Insatiable, Self-Directed Love Of Learning

When on their phones, Generation Z consumes three key types of content: inspiration (feeling motivated or interested, usually by example); education (learning or doing something new); and entertainment (zoning out while binging on YouTube or Netflix).

While they tend to associate positive emotions with inspiring and educational content, they tend to associate negative feelings with entertainment: after consuming entertainment content, they feel empty inside, even guilty about not spending their time in a more productive way.

One 19-year-old named Ashley told me, "Even when I relax, I like to feel like I'm doing something. Don't get me wrong, I love movies, but towards the end of a movie I always feel like I'm wasting my time." She told me that this is why she prefers gaming to watching movies, "Story games are kind of like movies in that they have plot twists. But in a game, I'm controlling the outcome. I'm part of the story. It feels like you're in it. You get to figure it out."

She went on to describe the thinking that happens during a game, telling me how you have to critically plan what to pick up, where to go, and if you make one decision versus another, there is a "butterfly effect" and the game ends in a different way. She told me this was the third time she was playing a specific game, and each time the outcome has been different.

Inspiring content motivates them to want to do something, be active for a cause, or better themselves or their world in some way. The most inspiring content for Generation Z comes through personalities they follow, mostly Instagramers and YouTubers. Once inspired, they move to learning.

They mostly use YouTube for content focused on learning, and they soak in hours of DIY and how-to videos, on basically any topic you can imagine. Here are a few examples of the types of videos they are watching:

How to…

- Code something
- Advance in a video game / computer game
- Apply makeup (for myself or others)
- Style or make clothing

- Learn a musical instrument

- Cook something

- Improve photography or digital editing skills

- Craft (e.g., how to make a pom pom rug or slime)

- Solve math problems

- Build a business (usually based on passive income)

- Write a great college essay

- Deal with a bully

- Get involved in activism, like ending school gun violence

YouTube videos are the primary source for learning, though some topics (for example, activism) might actually require search. Notice that learning something new is not necessarily tied to what kids are doing in school—it is anything they believe will help them accomplish a goal in their life, hobbies, or future career, or anything else.

It is clear that this is a generation that enjoys learning. On average, they watch YouTube videos 3 hours a day. Wow.

This generation assumes that whatever they need to learn, there will be a YouTube video up and waiting, an omnipresent education in their back pocket (likely bedazzled with jewels).

Interactive lessons often are watched in the moment they are needed, in the context while someone is taking action to create something or improve a skill. For example, Generation Z who like to bake may pull up a video on cake decorating once they are already in the kitchen with the cake made and tools out. In past generations, people would watch a cooking show or read a cookbook first, then later apply the recipe. This generation is pausing videos, doing things, and playing them again, going back and re-watching and re-trying. They are constantly learning, trying, doing.

Cognitive Outsourcing: Phones As a Part of Their Brains

For Generation Z, phones are an extension of their brains. This generation uses cognitive outsourcing to store facts and free up mental space for deep thinking. Historical dates? Periodic table elements? Math facts? "I don't have to remember this; I know where it is."

Generation Z is not the only generation who does this though. You do it too! Without your phone, can you remember your friends' numbers? Calendar appointments?

Learning With New Media And An App For Everything

Today's teens soak in information faster than ever before, and the most engaging ways of self-directed learning may just be in the new types of media that this generation has become accustomed to seeing and processing at incredible speeds. They think spatially and in 4D. The options to zoom, pinch, and swipe have always been available. 360 degree photography, ultra slow motion, and hi-speed video is standard. After years of scanning, scrolling, panning, clicking, swiping and gaming, this is how their brains are wired. Their attention spans are shorter, and you have a small window in which to capture their focus.

Generation Z spends significantly more time online than Millennials interacting with visual, video, and game content. They are far more interested in learning through videos than Millennials before them. In fact, 82 percent regularly use YouTube compared to 67 percent of Millennials. Almost half of Generation Z spend

3+ hours on YouTube per day, while this is true of less than a quarter of Millennials. 6 in 10 call YouTube their #1 preferred learning method[118].

But for the sake of my own children, I am absolutely not going to recommend that YouTube start passing out diplomas. Good grief! To me, some of the recommendations out there today implying that we should transform education into completely visual-based learning feels terrifying.

Just about every research study to date will tell you that this generation prefers visual content. Yes, yes, we get it. Connect through images to make your message visually digestible. The alphabet is *so* last century. I totally could have given you a 1-page infographic instead of writing this book and it would have communicated the same things. Right? Imagine teaching calculus or world history with nothing more than emojis. When you are teaching complex topics, sometimes you can't break every little thing down into something visual. It's just not realistic. And it is not reflective of how human beings learn. We also need to read it and hear it.

You might also hear a lot about how to turn your teaching material into snackable, bite-sized content—and that is true, at first. When presenting new content, Generation Z will learn best if you present a smorgasbord of inspiration. That way, they can decide on that perfect piece of gravlax with a mustard-dill sauce to indulge in. New media like Augmented Reality and Virtual Reality is perfect in this inspiration stage. Once that spark of inspiration hits and they get a taste, they will be hooked and ready to deep-dive into the topic.

Once inspired, they will watch every video, listen to every podcast, and (contrary to popular belief) read every article they can get their hands on to fulfill a knowledge gap. After all, this is a generation who loves to learn!

I know what you're thinking: Why don't I play videos on YouTube to get them hooked? Well, that's not exactly the method I'd suggest. For Generation Z, learning through videos is a self-directed activity. They will absorb more if they are doing that alone, at home. These students know that they can watch videos ad nauseam later. At school, they long for something different: in-person activities with classmates and teachers. Real connection. In fact, 6 in 10 cite in-person team-based activities as their preferred classroom learning method.[119]

Generation Z is 20 percent less likely than Millennials to prefer traditional textbooks. So what? Traditional textbooks are heavy—I'm with them on that one. With all the technology out there that allows a student to highlight and annotate and color code without having to lug around all the books and highlighters and sticky notes, who would go back to the old way?

Here is an example of how one study participant described the app she uses to read and take notes. With Generation Z, interruptions are constant, so it is interesting that she specifically mentions leaving and coming back to the right place as a main feature. In fact, during this video diary, she had several push notifications and reminders going off on her phone, even in just a few short minutes:

Notability is... on my iPad. And it's an app [that lets me] write on things. So I actually download the article, and I annotate that article and just highlight [and make notes on] really important stuff. And that helps me show what I was in the middle of. So if I have to stop for whatever reason, like if I'm doing it at school and I have to go to my next class, I'll just turn it off and then I will know exactly where I left off with my annotations because half of it will be highlighted and half of it won't. So that really, really helps me. I love

Notability. It's a great app for me. It helps me with a lot of my work.

This participant echoed a sentiment other participants said as well: they love taking notes. Um, what? Yes, you heard me right. Moreover, Generation Z takes notes on paper (with a real pen or pencil) 20 percent more than Millennials.

I love taking notes. And [Notability] honestly makes note-taking fun because you just get to have fun with it... You get to pick any color you want. You get to highlight in any color you want.... And it keeps me interested in taking notes in class, which I think is very important because then I'm actually interested in the class!

Apps are used prevalently to help with homework, especially in math. Just snap a photo of a math problem and woosh, problem solved, even for an algebraic equation:

What I do is, I have an app called Photomath, and I go to that. And, it usually takes a photo of any of the problems I'm looking for. So, if I choose to go to — let's say I go to my Memos, and I add a new one. Let's say I click two plus two, and I scan that. And it works just like that. Usually, if it doesn't have — if it does have variables, then I would put that in and it would figure out what x is [demonstrates an example on his phone] and it's negative two. But, usually it doesn't work with other symbols like theta or pi. Those questions are actually harder to look up on my phone. Because then I have to look for it specifically online, and it really doesn't help me like that. It only helps if I know what I need to find.... It doesn't help graph.... I usually have to go online

*and look for 'desmos graphing calculator'... and it would
help me find that out.*

We also heard about an app called Quizlet from nearly every high
schooler we spoke to about homework. This crowdsourced flashcard
app is populated by students taking the same classes. While they are
terrified of Wikipedia, this homework app is indispensable for them.

*Quizlet is one of the best homework-studying things that I
have. It's really, really good. I love Quizlet... Quizlet is probably my, like, main studying app. If I have a bio test coming
up, any test really, I would go to this app and I would just
search what I needed because honestly, it's made by people
that have been taking this class. It's not just a Wikipedia
from a 30-year-old man, just typing all the information you
have. It's based on your class. Like, it's really, really good.
And it's completely, I trust—Well, I don't trust everything
because it is made by other students. So I wouldn't exactly
just base it straight on the fact that, "Oh this is the defini-
tion for sure" because another student could have gotten it
wrong, so it's not 100 percent reliable and I definitely have
times where it's proved its unreliability. But [it's] a great tool
for me [especially when] I'm feeling lost. If I have a question
that I'm supposed to use the textbook for and I don't even
know where to look, like, what the keyword is I should even
be looking for in the textbook, I would go to Quizlet and
I would search up the thing, and just get a few keywords
about it, gather that stuff, and then I would go back in the
textbook. So gathering information, I definitely get a lot off
of Quizlet. If it was just about a text, if it was about a question, Quizlet is definitely my main homework-studying app.*

Generation Z is studying more because of crowdsourced tools like Quizlet. They're not just learning what you're teaching; they are learning what other teachers around the country are teaching:

> *Quizlet is everything to me... You can research anything and if you go to Chapter 14 AP Environmental Science, it gives you so many random things to study and it's like 'Oh, ok, look at all these terms.' I am in love with these. I print these out. I highlight these. I annotate these. I study these. I think they are so helpful because, yes, you can get all the study packets from your teacher, but also you need to take from another source... Yes, the teachers is giving you the test, but my teacher I know and definitely loves to play with us and put some random stuff on the test. Quizlet helps me prepare for that.*

Yes, the data in Quizlet could be wrong some of the time because it is created by humans. Washing machines can eat your socks once in a while, but you still use them. They are still a convenience. In the same way, crowdsourced tools are good resources most of the time. Instead of condemning these tools, we should be teaching our kids to fact check. We should be teaching them the framework to know that the information they are seeing is current, credible, and correct. We know that students are going to use crowdsourced information; fundamentally, the whole Internet is crowdsourced.

Another thing they love about tools like Quizlet and Kahoot! is the fact that these tools gamify learning. Answering questions is fun if it feels like a game, with music and timers and leaderboards.

This is how students today are studying and for the most part, learning the material. Why are we putting up barriers for them by telling them that if sometimes a site can be wrong, we shouldn't use it at all? That's not what they'll do in the real world, and it's not what you do either. You have a lingering cough? Dr. Google's there to diagnose you. Do you stick to WebMD only? Probably not. Why should they, then, when the information may be more digestible and in the exactly the right format somewhere else.

Generation Z enjoys gamified, crowdsourced learning because it matches their mental model and works in the way that they think. If we are going to be progressive educators, we need to work within that model.

A cornucopia of new mediums and new tools exists to supplement learning for today's youth. These tools are solving problems we did not even know were problems. They are making it quick and easy for students to pull out an iPad or phone or computer and go to exactly where they left off, to switch between these devices seamlessly, to find related topics and articles, to auto-play videos without even having to click. At the same time, Generation Z is spending more time learning. They are curious. They ask questions. They understand how to think critically. They love learning. Tools or no tools, isn't that what we ultimately want for our children?

Learning Is Social

Learning new skills has become a way to connect socially for this generation. This generation is made up of experts at finding online communities around specific topics. YouTube and Reddit are popular for this reason. While playing video games in your basement might seem to outsiders to be a solitary activity, it is actually one of the most social. Youth gamers constantly talk with each other through communication tools like Discord, stay in the know on Reddit threads, and watch, comment, and interact with other gamers on YouTube.

However, this generation is lonely. We know they are "connected" but they seem to be disconnected when it comes to each other. The number of teens who get together daily with friends just to hang out dropped by 40 percent from 2000 to 2015.

On top of that, we are seeing an unprecedented social erosion. In past generations, students had communities outside of school: neighbors, extended families, work friends, and church communities. Remember playing with the neighborhood kids? Well, Generation Z most likely does not do that. Less than 20 percent of kids today spend time with neighbors several times a week. In 1974, this was closer to 33 percent. Families are also becoming smaller, and children raised by a single parent has doubled from 15 percent to 31 percent in just 2 decades. Church communities are rapidly dwindling as well. Monthly church attendance has dropped by over 20 percent since 1970. We are also spending less time with friends from work. This has dropped from 2.5 hours a week in the mid-70s to under 1 hour today.[120]

Imagine a student being unhappy at school and having no other community to turn to.

57 percent of Generation Z students said they prefer in-person activities with classmates when learning in the classroom—21 percent more than reported by Millennials. 39 percent noted a preference for teacher-led instruction, while a whopping 78 percent respect teachers as "very important" to their learning and development.[121] While these digital natives are glued to their devices outside of the classroom, it seems that inside the classroom they may prefer more traditional methods of instruction. In looking at the data, I wonder

if these classroom learning preferences are a result of these teens and young adults not having other outlets for their in-person socialization that is so critical to our development as humans.

What They Are Not Getting: The Soft Side

While Generation Z is doing everything they can to beef up their hard skills inside of the classroom and on their own, a LinkedIn study found that corporate Human Resources and Learning and Development leaders who are observing Generation Z starting to enter the workforce contend that this group is lacking in their "soft" skills, such as communication skills, listening skills, and empathy 61 percent believe that Generation Z will need extra support for the development of soft skills as they navigate the workplace.[122]

This generation has been raised with substantially less face-to-face interaction. Social interactions are learned. They are honed by continual practice and feedback over time. If the majority of this generation's interactions are snaps and tweets and posts and texts, how will they ever learn how to act and interact appropriately in-person once they get to an office setting? This is a real concern.

A study by Deloitte suggests while Generation Z will bring an unprecedented level of technology skills to the workforce, organizational leaders, "express apprehension about their interpersonal communication skills." 84 percent of companies hiring Generation Z employees intended to double down on training of soft skills, namely communication, teamwork, and time management.[123] This is certainly an area where educators can focus their support.

Millennials and Generation Z are certainly different in behavioral patterns, but we can still learn from the skills that we now know Millennials were lacking when they got to the workplace. One workplace survey asked Millennials who are now corporate managers what aspects of leadership their education did not prepare them for, and nearly 1 in 3 cited conflict resolution.[124]

In a face-to-face conflict, Generation Z and Millennials alike do not seem to have the verbal words to express their perspective. On social media, they would know exactly what to say. As a result, many actively avoid in-person conflicts, and may even change jobs to find a better cultural fit. Our youth are going to extreme lengths to avoid in-person situations where conflict may arise, but conflict is not always avoidable. We need a better plan to teach conflict resolution tactics including active listening, empathy, and inclusion so that when they enter the workforce and interact with co-workers, they can interact in an empathetic way.

SPARK → DIVE → SHARE

The research conducted surrounding how Generation Z is learning with and without their mobile devices has revealed a pattern so consistent that I wonder if a new model of education could be developed on its foundation. Based on cognitive patterns of youth learning studied while they were on their own, it would be interesting to test and see if it would transfer to the classroom.

This model of learning centers on the idea that the most self-directed learning is kicked off by a spark of inspiration ("SPARK"). Once inspired, Generation Z goes into hyper-focus mode and will spend hours on their own deep diving into a topic ("DIVE"). If we let them do this on their on in a self-directed, rabbit-hole type of way, we can come back to the classroom ready to share knowledge and collaborate and work together to make, build, or solve something (SHARE).

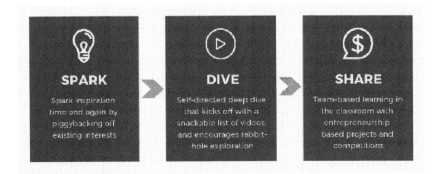

Too often we hear students talking about how boring school is. But the issue is not that they don't want to learn. They do—very much! Traditional education may seem to have lost its luster in large part because they are not getting the right inspiration trigger.

Here's the problem: because these youth are processing unprecedented amounts of information at faster speeds than ever before, their brains have evolved to make them cognitively more nimble to handle bigger mental challenges. But getting and keeping their attention is the hard part.

You have 8 seconds to capture attention. 8.

51 percent of students in 5th to 12th grade report being "not engaged" or "actively disengaged" at school. This is a big problem. Only 54 percent of college freshman and 61 percent of seniors felt challenged to do their best work.[125]

We know that once Generation Z decides they are interested, they are more driven to learn and can hyper-focus for extensive periods of time (think hours, not minutes). The question then becomes: how do we as educators spark that interest and send them into full-on "beast focus" mode?

(1) Spark Inspiration

We have data on what inspires youth: mostly powerful personal stories that make them want to take action for a cause or better themselves or their world in some way. In the past, teachers were supposed to walk into the classroom and provide a daily dose of super-inspiring stories. How exhausting to be constantly expected to spout inspiration every day that you show up. Is that even possible?

Putting this pressure on a teacher (even the best!) is unreasonable. We are humans, not robots. What's more, there is a whole Internet filled with inspiring stories, role models, amazing talks, and quotable images. If you can find a couple of these videos for each topic you cover in your classroom, you can spark interest again and again, with kids who are engaged and ready to learn. Spark an interest before even attempting to educate because to Generation Z, inspiration is such a positive feeling that it is worth hours scrolling and scrolling and scrolling to try to reproduce it. It provides a natural high that makes them want to dive in and explore everything around a topic.

This generation of self-starters, self-learners, and self-motivators will stop at nothing to make their mark on the world. That means there are three other more universal sparks you could be using as inspiration, sparks that nearly every Generation Z youth can rally for: (1) Money; (2) Entrepreneurship; (3) Social Causes.

For Millennials, culture is a key driver for learning a new skill in the workplace, but for Generation Z, money is king. In fact, 55 percent of Generation Z they would be willing to learn professional skills in exchange for a boost in pay from their job.[126]

According to an Inc article, "Educational attainment often looks different for entrepreneurial Gen Z."[127] Students who engage in projects and competitions related to starting businesses couple their natural entrepreneurial drive with an added team-based, social element to bolster learning. Participants in these types of programs have gone on to earn 50 percent more than their peers, and 25 percent have gone on to start at least one business.[128]

Feed Generation Z's curiosity. Tap into the entrepreneurial spirit. Make stuff and help Gen Z make stuff. Collaborate with them and help them collaborate with others. Educate and build expertise, they want to be experts. Help them to achieve it. Don't talk down to Generation Z; treat them as adults. Inspire your audience with social causes to rally behind and fight for. Assume they have opinions and are vocal, because truly they do.

(2) Dive Deeply

After the initial spark comes the deep dive. Seth Godin pioneered the idea of flip-teaching in a TED talk nearly a decade ago. If you have not seen his TED talk, you too will be inspired: https://youtu.be/sXpbONjV1Jc.

Since then, we have tested flipping and while it works especially well for some subjects like math, for other subjects it is not quite there.

Instead of simply flipping, try frontloading. Good inquiry comes from knowledge. If you want to turn a lecture into a discussion, ask students to watch YouTube videos—or research however they would like—ahead of time, before you really start digging into the topic in class. Let them dig into it on their own, which will lead to more conversation and deeper learning in the classroom. With a little knowledge, they can come to class ready to discuss, collaborate, solve problems together, and build things.

Maybe it is all those YouTube how-to videos they are watching late at night, but nearly half of Generation Z learners prefer a self-directed and independent approach when learning something for the first time.

This Generation has been doing Internet research since they were practically in the womb, so perhaps it comes as second nature. Perhaps they just want to do this deep dive alone so they can have space to think it through. Either way, one thing is worth trying: have them do the bulk of the learning, with bite-sized, self-directed deep-dive research. As a generation who despises anything slow, micro-learning may be an answer here. Used frequently in companies to quickly close skill gaps, this bite-sized education may fit better into the busy lives of Generation Z. Since 52 percent use YouTube or social media for typical research assignments anyway, this method taps into the tools they are already using and the habits they have already created.

This generation represents the ultimate consumers of snack media. They communicate in bite-sized, punchy headlines and razor-sharp text with no fluff. Be careful about thinking that simple equates to uninformed, though, as there can be a great deal of nuance in the short and sweet. Generation Z communicates in symbols, emoticons, and emojis. With symbols providing context and subtext for their conversations, there is no need to add extra words. While great at rapid-fire banter, precision communication is not their forte. Symbols are easier than massaging words and it enables Generation Z to leave room for interpretation.

By inviting Generation Z to research and find their own content on whatever topic you are teaching, you are treating them with respect, intelligence, and the independence they need to continue to grow. You are helping them become experts through "snackable" content they find, select, and consume on their own.

(3) Share & Collaborate With Teammates

This is the time to come back to the classroom for the learning; this is where the real magic happens. As the guide, you facilitate and direct discussion among students who are sharing the deep dive research they found the night before. Give them questions to think about, and in teams help them work a problem, solve a social issue, build something, or create a business.

Based on this model, a different kind of success metric might be needed to judge how effective your learning is. Perhaps we start asking our students:

- SPARK: How inspired did you feel?
- DIVE: Did you research on your own, outside of the classroom, beyond what your teacher asked?
- SHARE: Did you learn anything relevant to your life or future possible career?

While these ideas are just that—ideas, untested hypotheses based on the data—the bottom line is that Generation Z is soaking up information in new ways. In order to get educational messages to stick in their minds, we need to start thinking about how to adapt teaching styles to this generation's new patterns and mental models of thought.

The Hard Part: Finding That Balance

For educators and parents alike, the phone seems amazing and frightening at the same time. It creates new lines of thought and 4D problem solving. But at the same time, it is killing social and emotional development in our children. It is clear that we must attempt to find a balance find a balance between: (a) working in the way your students are already thinking—in the way their brains process information—to aid in learning; and (b) to ensure that we're teaching kids to effectively interact with each other, with plenty of opportunity for social interaction.

I feel for educators out there because finding a balance between these is really hard. These two opposing demands, along with kids who need something different each year, make it nearly impossible to structure a repeatable way to find this balance. It will be constantly changing.

In the past, progressive educators have wanted to be a "guide on the side", not a "sage on the stage." But it is not reasonable to sit next to every child coaching them individually in every moment of your lesson. You do not scale. Technology does. The zone of proximal development shifts from you to their phones. Knowing this, you can use technology in strategic ways to be that personal guide.

We know that we should be using technology when it authentically deepens the learning experience (and not use technology for technology's sake). We also know that as today's youth use technology to grow in new ways, they sacrifice other types of growth. So how do we find a balance?

There are three types of things we should be considering: Right tech? Right Application? Right balance?

Is it the right tech? One school in Utah has a 3D model that prints a heart. So cool! But... wouldn't an augmented reality or virtual reality experience be more valuable? Imagine if they could do surgery in a virtual capacity. Which would truly deepen the learning?

Is it the right application? If your school does have a 3D printer, instead of printing hearts, what if we had students designing instruments, printing them out, and experimenting with them? And what if we coupled this with an integrated approach with a business class and enabled them to write a business plan for their new instrument? What if they could couple this with English and write a technical paper on it?

Is it the right balance? What other soft skills can we be teaching alongside the technology that we're choosing to use, to enhance the whole child? Communications? Problem Solving? Teamwork?

I doubt you will find an educator who is going to suggest technology for technology's sake. It should be used only when it impacts the learner or sparks interest so that the learner understands something in a new or deeper way.

Teachers, I want you to remember that you are AMAZING. You have a huge responsibility to shape our next generation, and the fact that you are reading this, trying to work with the new way that this generation thinks in order to be a better teacher, brings me great hope for our future leaders. Thank you for choosing this noble profession. Thank you for taking a chance learning from someone who's never taught in a high school classroom. Thank you for being you.

5 TAKEAWAYS FOR EDUCATORS

1. **Creatively spark interest:** There is no better time to be an educator than today because this generation truly loves to learn! Creatively spark their interests with powerful human stories and multiple options they can choose from in order to set them on the path for deep learning to occur. This generation has a real super-power when it comes to blocking out distractions and hyper-focusing, once they are interested. Let's tap into that.

2. **Provide space to deep dive:** Once you spark that interest, give your students space and independence to deep dive on their own. Self-directed, snackable learning is what this generation does best. Longer class periods may be effective here.

3. **Focus on hands-on activities in class:** In the classroom, focus on in-person, team-based activities to make the content "stick" in their minds. Craft activities centered around entrepreneurship projects and social activism to ensure they stay interested.

4. **Amp up the soft skills:** Whenever possible, emphasize the importance of learning soft skills. This is the one area where this generation is severely lacking once they enter the workforce.

5. **Encourage connection:** This generation needs it more than any before it. Anything you can do to facilitate the building of communities within your school will prove essential to this lonely generation of youth.

5 TAKEAWAYS FOR MARKETERS

1. **Incorporate education into your marketing strategy:** Generation Z loves learning and feels that time invested in learning a new skill is worth it. Make sure they are aware that: (a) they are learning; and (b) the skill is or will be useful to them.

2. **Use a person to connect:** Consider a brand ambassador or YouTube personality to compliment your skill-based marketing, as this generation connects more with people, not brands.

3. **Spark → Dive → Share:** While this cycles applies to marketers in a slightly different way, but still applies. For marketers, your introductory step here would be to spark inspiration. Once interest has been sparked and your potential customers engaged, you must offer original, compelling content across multiple channels. Finally, you can encourage these customers—now that you've helped them become experts—to create or

co-create content with you. This could even be done through monetary-based competitions to tap into Generation Z's money-centered worldview.

4. **More visual and interactive content:** Generation Z's relationship with technology is rewiring how they show up as consumers. Gamification, crisp visuals, bite-sized (1-2 minute) videos, and razor-sharp taglines are good bets for sparking that inspiration.

5. **Find the right balance:** Technology is creating new ways of thinking. Phones are part of students' brains today and banning them from the classroom would be like taking away a piece of their brains. At the same time, all the technology they consume is having an impact on their social and emotional wellbeing. Find a balance in the classroom by determining if it's the right tech, if it's the right application of the tech, and if there are other skills we could be teaching alongside the tech. Find that balance!

PART III: THE NEW RULES

In my childhood, I always wondered why my Grandma Nucci's lasagne tasted better than any other. The ingredients were no different than anyone else's—pasta, ricotta, mozzarella, marinara, eggplant, ground beef. And yet, somehow, when she baked it in her kitchen in her special lasagne pan, it magically transformed into a plate of pure love.

My mother and I affectionately deemed it a result of "the magic pan," but over the years, I have come to believe it was her skillfully-honed packing technique. Grandma Nucci was able to take the same ingredients and yet layer them in a unique way that perfectly fit in her pan so that, once baked, she made certain that each morsel was filled with just the right balance of flavor.

In the same way, these trends about Generation Z are just that—trends. Like all generations, Generation Z has a unique set of defining characteristics. Marketers need to understand how these traits impact their preferences for connecting, communicating, learning, and transacting. At this point, though, you may know enough to win the Gen Z edition of HQ Trivia, but that's it.

You Have The Ingredients.

But now is the time for the perfect layering to begin. From an anthropological perspective, I love hanging out with teenagers. They fascinate me and entertain me and I was thrilled to have the opportunity to write 45,000 words on their digital idiosyncrasies. But now is the time to move on from that and start applying these trends to you and your business, your brand! Yes, it's exciting! This is where the real magic happens.

As you were reading past sections of this book, I am sure you were asking yourself: How do I apply this to my situation? How do I take these general trends and make them relevant to me, my company, my products? How do I transform these trends into evidence-based decision making? What can I do with this information? How do I prioritize opportunities, given my resources, to respond to this shift in marketing? Knowing that a set of bright-eyed marketers would be doing exactly this, I added takeaways at the end of each trend I wrote about to assist you as you started to apply the concepts.

In this part of the book—the most crucial part, in my opinion—I walk you through these very questions in more depth. This is where you get to explore not just the trends but the *rules* of marketing to this generation. You know your customer best, and by working through this section and critically thinking about and answering the questions outlined by each rule, you will create the basis for your fresh, new marketing strategy.

Answering these questions for your company may not be easy. You may feel at times that you're drinking from the firehose and you couldn't possibly implement everything discussed or recommended here. That's ok. This is your next step: a crucial step in which you will need to work through these questions to find out how you can successfully market to a huge future demographic that is driven by technology and more detached from brand loyalty than any generation ever before.

To jog your creative juices and help you start thinking about how you will apply these principles, I have provided a number of ideas and scattered stories throughout—examples of companies who have successfully applied these techniques, often in very creative ways. I know that many of my readers are in B2B organizations, and some books ignore this crowd. That is not what you're going to get here! Please note that I am intentionally using examples from both B2B and B2C organizations because I firmly believe that it is essential for both types of companies to alter their strategies in order to survive and thrive with this new generation. Let's map out a plan to layer these uniquely for your company.

Let the layering begin!

RULE #1: SPARK INSPIRATION

Of everything I have learned in my research, the most fascinating to me about Generation Z is their incredible ability to hyper-focus for hours on end, once inspired to do so. They scroll and triage, scanning for nothing more than a spark of inspiration to strike, as hurricanes of information rush past them. The moment that inspiration hits, though, down the rabbit hole they go, learning and absorbing everything they can. Wouldn't this be amazing if they were learning about your brand in this way?

Time and again we see a predictable pattern of Spark → Dive → Share. As a marketer for either B2C or B2B, your biggest challenge is to spark inspiration (Spark), to capture their attention with an interesting or engaging visual or video that causes them to click. At that point, you have about 8 seconds to hook them. If you can succeed in that, this generation goes full-on social media stalker mode and will deep dive for hours (Dive). Once they learn what they can, they feel like they are experts enough to start sharing. They will seek out online communities, talk with their friends, and even create Instagram accounts specifically curated for these topics so they can stay informed (Share).

For marketers, the most daunting step here is to get past the noise and spark that zing of inspiration. Generation Z checks social media feeds around 100 times a day. Apart from when they are in class, these youth are constantly scrolling and scanning. Generation

Z multitasks to such a degree that their brains have actually evolved to allow for a greater ability to process visual stimuli. As marketers, we must be more strategic in terms of how we capture attention, or we will see a lot of wasted money on social media campaigns that do not stick with this audience.

The best way to do this is to find out what ignites your target audiences, and tap into their existing interests. The results of tailored customer research should give you a range of ideas to try in terms of associating your brand with a hobby, interest, or personality your customers actively follow on social media. From there, you can A/B test your campaigns to see what ignites your tribe.

Imagine you are a company selling a music product or service. Maybe there is a certain artist that your audience follows. If you can associate your brand with a person, that's great, but this can be done even when there is no direct link. In fact, it can even be better to go with a unique and unexpected partnership. By pooling resources and different (but complementary) audience networks, unlikely brands can collaborate and achieve much more than they could have alone.

Remember when budget-friendly Hyundai Motors was able to redefine "luxury vehicle" by partnering with Prada? Among other enhancements, the Genesis interiors were replaced with spot Saffiano leather, the leather that Prada bags are known throughout the world for. Coupled with a smart social media strategy, Prada's revenues sky-rocketed by 6 percent over the course of a year.[129]

I don't know about you, but if I were a socially-focused Generation Z traveling to Asheville, NC, I know what hotel I'd be staying in: McKibbon Hospitality hotel. Want to know why? Because of their partnership with animal rescue organization Charlie's Angels. One adorable pup who needs a home lives at each of McKibbon's hotels and stays there until he or she is adopted. What a joy it is to see these adorable puppies adopted on social media:

Unique partnerships, especially those associated with a cause, may be just the ticket for your brand to create something unusual and worthy of Generation Z's attention.

Of course, knowing what your customers are interested in is great. But what if you knew their moods too—at any given moment? You can absolutely reinvigorate an old campaign with new knowledge of customers. Snickers got real creative when it decided to couple AI technology with customer research to give the Snickers' "Hungry? Why Wait?" campaign a new life. They partnered with MIT and Google to create an algorithm that predicted the most "hangry" people on social media using a combination of traffic, news, and weather. These people received coupons for Snickers bars directly, along with directions to their nearest 7-Eleven—leading to an increase in Snickers' sales by nearly 70% and an explosion in social media engagement.

Often a choice in what to see is all it takes. Generation Z is more independent than their predecessors. Give the user the perception of control by offering choices in posts, stories or inspiration. If they feel like they can personalize their experience, it often results in increased engagement.

In this example, the TED website asks directly, "What inspires you?" and offers options to quickly choose from.

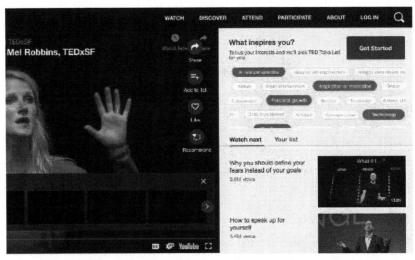

Source: Screenshot from www.ted.com, March 2019.

For Generation Z, the perception of control and personalization is one of the most compelling attributes of Instagram. Setting what topics or personalities to follow on feeds like Instagram or Google News or any other feed is a favorite feature of this generation, though surprises outside of those parameters can be delightful and engaging.

Inspiration is Generation Z's single-most communicated reason for going to feeds like Instagram and Pinterest, but this is true for other feeds as well. As a whole, Generation Z derives inspiration from personalized feeds. The question has shifted from "What do I want" to "What should I want", and this generational cohort relies on recommendations engines to feed them suggestions on what to be interested in.

If you want to be top of mind, you need to be noticed. And to be noticed, you need to show up on their social feeds.

ASK YOURSELF...

- For the content we have published today, what is most inspiring?

- For the content we have published today, what is most engaging?

- For the content we have published today, what stands out from the noise? What falls flat?

- Of the people who are engaging with my content, are they the right audiences?

- What is my brand missing in its content?

- How could I make my content zing?

- How can we give our users more choice or control over what they see?

- What new types of content should I be thinking about when planning?

- Who are my top customers, and what are they interested in, aside from my brand?

- If I'm not sure, what kind of research will I need to do to find out? When will I start?

RULE #2: INCORPORATE LEARNING INTO YOUR MARKETING STRATEGY

Time-obsessed Generation Z feels guilty after indulging in content designed for the sole purpose of entertainment because they feel like they should be spending their time in more productive ways. For this generation, marketers should shift their strategy toward learning, a topic they feel good about. It does not matter what kind of learning it is—this generation is excited to learn new skills, absorbing knowledge they didn't have before.

Many brands assume that youth are glued to entertaining video, and often adopt the strategy of advertising during popular series on streaming services, or advertising while someone is watching a sports game or checking sports scores. But the question you as a brand should be asking yourself is this:

Do you want to associate your brand with feelings of guilt for time wasted on entertainment or with feelings of accomplishment as something is learned?

Some brands may wish to tap into this feeling of guilt. For H&R Block or TurboTax, it might be extremely effective to advertise quick services while someone is already feeling a little guilty. When a user is already feeling like a sloth for watching a show, they might be motivated to start today on their taxes because they may be feeling guilty about procrastinating on their taxes as well.

However, for most brands, you would do better to be associated with positive feelings of empowerment and achievement that come when this generation learns something new.

This is one of those strategies that could be readily adopted by B2B companies. If a buyer is watching a video on YouTube related to learning a work skill, it could be effective to advertise your service. For instance, say a busy project manager who read and loved this book decided to watch a vlog on my YouTube channel. It might be effective to advertise project management software to them at that time (hint, hint, wink, wink).

Another strategy is to not go with ads at all, and instead create and advertise a series of learning videos or podcasts as a part of your integrated marketing strategy. Let's go with the same example of a project management software company. They could do a vlog series on YouTube or LinkedIn (which does not have a high percentage of Generation Z using it right now but likely will in a few years once more of them have entered the workforce).

Generation Z loves learning and feels that time invested in learning a new skill is worth it. Make sure they are aware that: (a) they are learning; (b) the skill is or will be useful to them; (c) specifically what brand is teaching them the skill (their multitasking brain may need a reminder—don't be subtle).

Another great B2B strategy is to sponsor conferences in order to associate your brand with learning. Make sure you have cool swag when you go, as Generation Z cares more about things than Millennials!

The point here is that inspiration and learning are perceived as being worth Generation Z's time. Entertainment is not. While they do watch entertainment based programs and videos and you can certainly find them there, they feel guilty about it afterward. Consider this when choosing where to place your ads or planning your content calendar.

ASK YOURSELF...

- How much of my brand's marketing is associated with entertainment? Learning?

- Do I want my brandmore associated with guilt or accomplishment? (Not a trick question! It is a decision you should make)

- What types of learning-based marketing should we consider?

- Which learning content creators could/should my brand pair with?

- What learning content could/should we create?

- Learning content takes time to develop: what can I do today to move this idea forward?

- What else do I need to know about my customers before moving forward? How could I do that research?

- What is my next step?

RULE #3: CONNECT WITH PEOPLE

Know a teenager who is into beauty or fashion? Ask what sources they follow. Go ahead, text your niece right now... I'll wait.

You might be expecting these types of answers: YouTube, Instagram.

But instead, this is what you'll hear: James Charles; Jeffree Star.

If you ask Generation Z what "sources" they follow, they will name people!

When influencers talk about brands, people listen. This is the basic principle that has made influencer marketing take off. Social networks are growing, and the generation that grew up using them is reaching buying maturity. With a real job and actual income of their own, they will be clicking through Instagram and other social networks and buying products they see. However, this also means that there are more people than ever on social media in general (each with lots of curated accounts), which leads to a whole lot of uniquely branded user-generated content, resulting in a whole lot of noise.

If you can cut through the noise, boosting your brand engagement with influencer marketing has never been more reasonable: forget massive influencers and microinfluencers. Nanoinfluencers with only 1,000 followers or more have become increasingly popular, especially for local brands. For a small commission, they are willing to say just about anything you want about your product, and they tend to be easier to work with. Hiring multiple nanoinfluencers instead of relying on a single big-time creator may make your brand seem like it is all over the place in a more natural way. You will appear within reach for the everyday consumer, a value that Generation Z highly admires.

User-generated content (UGC) is quickly seeping into other types of marketing content including emails, product-display pages, and other ad campaigns. Brands have started to use a mix of professional photos and user-generated ones on these different channels to blend professional with authentic. Here is an example of this from a Munchkin email marketing campaign:

Source: UGC in Munchkin emails, created by Pixlee.

User-generated content does not have to come from influencers. Garmin is a great example of a brand that incorporates its customer stories into its Instagram posts, and it garners goodwill and engagement every time it does. It recently even put up a Story Highlight for customer stories labeled "From You." It takes very little effort to showcase customer stories on Instagram, and it typically results in high engagement and organic social media growth every time. Don't forget to tag your customer in the post!

If you do go with paid influencer marketing, a true story and authentic photo trumps a product picture anyday. Here is an example from @bridiewilkins who brings up the sponsoring product in a natural way: "Are you an over packer or under packer? I brought 11 bikinis with me for 5 days in Dubai so I think you can guess which I am… Tap to see where this beauty is from #ad #swimwear365."

A number of companies try this but cannot seem to get it right. Here is an influencer marketing campaign by Wells Fargo in the form of a story. It looks like it follows the rules, yes. But it fails for a few key reasons. First, it was clearly not written by @jigglebeatmedia. When you look at the length, punctuation, and capitalization, it is all wrong. It is not on-brand for her. Her wall is speckled with photos and videos of half-naked jiggling butts and half-naked sculpted abs. This pristinely-posed, fully-clad professional photo screams stock image. Even if this is her, in contrast to the rest of the content she posts, it feels phony. Your Generation Z audience can make a gut decision about marketing speak in a nanosecond. Make sure that if you spend the money on influencer marketing, it reads authentic and on-point for both you and the influencer.

Influencer marketing is not just influencers taking photos of products. On the contrary, some of the best campaigns are related to learning and doing. When Fiji water partnered with fashion blogger

Danielle Bernstein @weworewhat, she and trainer Eric Johnson created a series of 8-minute paid workout videos called bodyworewhat, a spinoff of her handle. This campaign offered 25% off your first home shipment of Fiji water so you stay hydrated while you work for that summer body.

For B2C brands selling products with mass consumer appeal, influencer marketing is a no-brainer. Yet for B2B brands, it is not as easy. B2B buyers do not typically click on a link from an Instagram post, go to a website, and purchase something right then and there. B2B sales are more likely based on word-of-mouth and personal relationships. The dollar amount is higher but the sales cycle is much longer. The average sales cycle for enterprise software, for example, is 6 months. Buyers can spend months researching and asking questions before they purchase.

That said, content shared or created by influencers provided 11 times higher return on investment than the average display ad after 12 month, and 92 percent of marketers that used influencer marketing claimed it is effective at reaching audiences.[130] So it is definitely worth it if you can find the right B2B influencer to partner with who aligns to your brand. But identifying the right B2B influencers is not easy. Many marketers use just one data point to determine which group of influencers to engage with: reach (how large their social community is across all digital channels). While reach is important, there are other metrics to consider as well including relevance (measures how consistently is the influencer's content "on topic" for your brand), resonance (measures engagement and how far shared content travels), and reference (interactions with other influencers).[131]

Today, many in B2B collaborate with influencers to create branded content like eBooks. The great news is that this media lives forever, indexed in Google. Advocates of this method say that the advantage of creating long-form content is that you can leverage smaller pieces of the asset for social media amplification, kind of like making your Thanksgiving leftovers into snacks for the days to come. Yet for this new generation of visual youth entering the workforce, I would recommend video content over text, and video snippets for bite-sized, shareable social content. Generation Z was practically born searching for information online. They are extremely sensitive to the feeling of being "sold to." I promise you won't wow them with fancy text. Instead, don't sell to them; talk with them or teach them something new. Seeing your face will make them feel more connected to you. Generation Z craves real connection, so ditch the eBook. It is possible you will never have to write a "slick sheet" ever again either.

For B2B, there are some marketers who believe that partnering with a long-term brand ambassador may be a more successful form of influencer marketing, especially if that influencer is actually creating original content instead of just sharing.[132] While I have not seen metrics to support this, it makes sense if sponsored learning-based content from a long-term brand ambassador is in your plan.

We have been talking about people here, and I want to make sure we are not skipping over people who directly contribute to your band story: *your* people. Generation Z is seeking deeper connections all around, and one of the biggest draws of your brand just might be the people they get to interact with, or the people involved behind the scenes of our business. Your employees represent your band. There is a reason that Zappos goes to such lengths to hire its customer service reps (even going so far as to pay them to leave after their initial training): because they are unique, quirky souls who contribute to the Zappos brand in every single interaction you have with one of them. This is critical for both B2C and B2B, but especially B2B who may have many more interactions prior to purchase.

How do you showcase your people? Here is a phenomenal example from Amazon: https://youtu.be/x-fyLCM_0Y4

Yes, put down this book for a moment and go watch it! Amazon is an enormous company and people do not typically interact with employees there unless they are calling a help center. This video, then, is a brilliant way to humanize the behemoth company and inject light-hearted fun into its brand personality.

ASK YOURSELF...

- How do I communicate my brand's promise through people?

- How should we involve influencers in our marketing?

- Which influencers is our audience following? Which align to our brand?

- How should we use customer stories? How would we find them? Where would we feature them?

- How can I highlight my employees as a part of the brand?

- How can I make customer service a differentiator?

RULE #4: BUILD COMMUNITIES ONLINE AND OFFLINE

Generation Z customers long for real connection. Though this generation is "connected" more than ever before, they are increasingly disconnected when it comes to face-to-face interaction. Social skills are learned—practiced and honed over time—and Generation Z is not getting this practice. For marketers, or really anyone in this workforce, this should be a terrifying prospect, especially when you consider how much of today's business revolves around relationship-building. Given the paucity of social skills among this generation, it will no doubt become an even more critical skill than ever before.

Teens certainly have fun at in-person events—and why wouldn't they? Humans of all ages need face-to-face social interaction to stay in good mental health. But they are so addicted to their phones that they postpone going, even somewhere *lit*. They need one more level in that game with the cliffhanger. Or they have to post one more Instagram story because they've got *tea to spill* or they're *firing shots*. Or maybe they are just so exhausted from the constant scrolling—and sleep deprivation from the constant scrolling—that they wind up *draking*, moping around in an emotional mess, not wanting to go out or do anything (*real talk:* not something that average teenagers should be feeling). *Zayum!* That is a lot of Generation Z slang, all in one paragraph.

Human beings are social creatures, and it is important for the future health of this generation that in-person communities are not replaced entirely by social media.

As a marketer, we often think about building and growing online communities—and that is still a good strategy. Invest in creating communities for your customers who share specific interests related to your brand, or who are interested in learning a particular skill. This will not only build brand engagement, but also help to connect these teens with a tribe, as they are not getting as much social connection elsewhere in their lives.

But what we can do alongside these digital communities is offer in-person events to maximize your impact. Even knowing that an in-person group is nearby might be enough for a Generation Z youth to know that they are not alone. NaNoWriMo is an example of an organization that does this beautifully. Every November, this non-profit organizes National Novel Writer's Month where 300,000 writers have 30 days to reach 50,000 words. This group establishes a robust online community, daily motivation by email, and online words of wisdom from famous authors. More than that, it sets up live write-ins at community centers and libraries across the country.

WW (formerly Weight Watchers) represents a business successfully implementing this pairing as a paid model. Even on an in-person ("studio") plan, subscribers have access to an impressive app that offers communities, feeds, and (of course) food. This example is especially powerful when you understand how they structured their digital communities for learning new skills, combined these online communities with in-person ones, and linked themselves with a top-of-mind social cause: lifestyle health and wellness (not weight loss).

As a part of this rebranding strategy, they offered teens as young as 13 free memberships as a response to the chilling stats on childhood obesity. While that part ended up being controversial, one thing is for sure: WW looked at this new generation of customers and modeled their structure based on all of the core principles we have been talking about here. Imagine what more they could do with increased YouTube videos or accountability partnerships in the form of a Snapchat streak or gamified point counting! The possibilities to build from here are endless.

One thing that many companies are quickly learning is that they cannot just say they are industry leaders: they have to look the part within the social ecosystem. B2B friends: this applies to you too. What may be most frightening for today's brands about Generation Z is their inherent understanding of the Internet's nonverbal language. If your website is not optimized for mobile, or your logo or profile pic or header image looks dated, or if you are not consistently posting all the right junk in all the right places (Meghan Trainor, anyone?) it does not matter what your message is—you look old. You must become a part of the conversation. To organically grow or boost engagement, you have to become a part of this conversation. Find accounts with whom your brand might be a good fit, and start to like posts and add comments. Engage with your followers, follow up on replies, and you will become a part of the conversation.

For WW, this involves quickly replying to and following up on each question on Instagram. After showing a recipe, WW responded to customer questions about its point value:

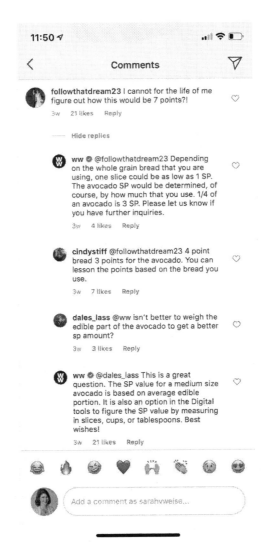

In this example, WW has chosen to post directly. While great for Millennials, this will not be as effective for Generation Z, who develops relationships more with people than with brands. Instead, what about a consistent community manager who responds on behalf of the brand? This adds a human element to your brand, and is more effective for the Generation Z audience. This is especially relevant for B2B companies, which often tend to feel more corporate, less human.

Speaking of B2B, in-person events like networking breakfasts, conferences, and trade shows have always been popular. Yet in this climate of less frequent in-person experiences, they are apt to be even more critical to make your brand stand out. Go to these events with the goal of making genuine connections. So forget the online conference and plan an in-person version. The long-lasting success of your business will be a function of relationship building, in a world that often fails to support this.

For B2C, events are great for you too. This could be anything from a fashion show to social activism based on the goals of your campaigns and the interests of your customers.

ASK YOURSELF...

- How can I improve or grow my company's digital communities?

- How can we make real, in-person connections?

- What will we get out of better relationships?

- What has stopped us in the past from doing this?

- What research do I need?

- What events could I plan? Who would be there? What would they get out of it?

- What is this dependent on?

- What can I do today to move this forward?

RULE #5: QUALITY CONTENT... PRETTY, WITH VIDEO

While Millennial teens primarily use social media to keep up with friends, Generation Z sees social media as a hub for content consumption. This is very good for brands like yours because it means that if you create great content and can get it in front of them, they will engage. Focus on creating quality content geared toward inspiration or learning.

Once your brand is noticed, you must have sufficient content in enough different places to make the scavenger hunt real. If you go through the hurdles of getting your brand to be noticed, you must provide enough content for someone to find. It is truly delightful to your prospective customers when they are on their tenth app or website and they find something new—a little golden nugget—an unseen video or an exclusive story. Go to where your customers are.

Are they scrolling for hours on Instagram? Watching video after video of certain channels on YouTube? Are they already looking for specific content... Makeup tutorials? Livestreams of James Charles? Gaming playthroughs? E3 event coverage? Go there. Go where your customers are. Find out what your specific audience does, and use that to your advantage. If you know that your customers are spending hours a day watching YouTube videos on gaming, go to YouTube and either sponsor an influencer in that space or create your own original content.

Modern lifestyles and constant digital consumption are preventing Generation Z from getting adequate sleep, inciting stress and creating an opportunity for brands to provide solutions. If you know your users are watching your videos late at night, you must also assume that they will likely fall asleep to autoplay. Content is the name of the game here: ensure that you have enough videos to enable autoplay for hours. You can even try sponsoring sleep stories or labeling some of your channels as nighttime videos. So give your customers enough content on your channel to dream sweet dreams of your brand.

Quality content is still the name of the game for Generation Z. As marketers continue to blast noise on social media, today's youth are growing weary of the surface-level nonsense. Bad content, however, can have pronounced negative consequences for brands. According to research by Adobe, 71 percent of consumers reported that they would not buy from a brand that pushes content that is poorly written, irrelevant, or poorly designed.[133] Generation Z prioritizes true and authentic messaging as much as they do articulate and well-designed copy. They rely on content creators to provide quality content that inspires, educates, and brings people together as a community.

But get this: your content does not always have to be fresh. B2B managers, look alive! Because for skill-based learning, Generation Z is just as interested in evergreen articles, as long as they are still relevant to the task at hand. They certainly like to follow YouTubers and watch their videos, often in order (similar to binge-watching multiple seasons of your favorite show). But as long as the content is not outdated nor the products old, Generation Z will soak in the content. "Cute is cute," one fashion-loving participant told me. If this products being reviewed are old and you cannot buy them anymore, that ruins the review though. For example, if a customer is watching older beauty videos, they may become frustrated that they are not able to buy the same makeup anymore. If you wish to repurpose this type of content anyway, there is an easy fix: add an interaction on top of the video an alternate product, or write this in your video description and in the comments.

Where should you post this content? Not everywhere, please. Generation Z has its own rules of etiquette when it comes to where to post different types of content. You'll look like a novice (or worse yet, a Millennial!) if you post everything, everywhere. I know it is tempting when you are using social media management tools that make it is so easy. But resist the urge. Post inspiration and professional, edited, beautiful slice-of-life photos on Instagram. Post behind-the-scenes, exclusive footage on Snapchat. Post professional announcements (like a new podcasts posted or a new blog post) on Twitter. On YouTube, post tutorial, review/opinion, DIY videos. Find out what your specific audience does, and use that to your advantage. If you know that your customers are spending hours a day watching YouTube videos on skincare routines, take your content to YouTube or create new content with the help of existing influencers.

Also, remember that email is not dead. This is still a channel for you—a major one at that! Social media has an opportunity for better, bigger engagement than email. While an email will never go "viral", it is an effective communication strategy because it is used habitually by Generation Z. It should be combined as a part of an integrated marketing strategy for a consistent base of awareness and e-commerce, if that applies to you.

So I'm sure by now you're thinking: "Ok, ok. I know where to put my content. But what do I create in the first place? Give me some rules about that." Here goes—

Let's talk about videos because YouTube is very likely the place where Generation Z will discover you. Generation Z watches hours of videos a day. Hours! Increase traffic to your YouTube channel and give your page a sharp, curated look by making sure your channel is organized in a clear way to keep visitors engaged with interesting, easy to find videos. Organize your videos into playlists, grouping them by topic. According to iMatrix, "This improves the likelihood of driving traffic to additional videos in your playlist due in large part to YouTube's video search algorithm."[134] Add keyword-rich titles and descriptions to both your videos and playlists, targeting keywords using YouTube's Keyword Suggestion Tool as a reference. Adding a detailed description gives you another 5,000 words with which to add beneficial keywords to help YouTube's algorithm understand who you are and what you provide on your channel.

On YouTube the visuals are important. Use channel art to echo your branding, and carefully select thumbnails for your videos that communicate the value the viewer will get from the video and also tie into your brand image.

On Instagram, crisp visuals, 1-2 minute bite-sized videos, and razor-sharp taglines are good bets on sparking that inspiration Generation Z expects from this platform. Focus on the design of your page, the consistency of images, and the photo array on your brand's page. Grabbing the attention of visual Generation Z consumers takes eye-catching graphic design on both social media posts and in video. Consumers respond favorably to branded content that is authentic, well designed and relevant. Because social media is mostly visual for Generation Z, design plays a major role. When you look at influencer profiles on Instagram, nearly all look professionally designed and managed by brand guidelines with specific colors and font choices—and there is an excellent reason why. 46 percent said that strongly branded content that provides a good experience influences their purchasing decisions, and 24 percent said they would share it with their friends.

With all this content now comes the task to organize it. As born aggregators, Generation Z will love any lists and category groupings you throw at them. Try contests on Instagram and/or Pinterest to encourage brand engagement to co-create lists. Show your customers that you are organized too: On Instagram, create story highlights to categorize the types of content you provide. Give viewers a reason to follow you. Encourage sharing, not just of posts, but of collections. Regularly schedule lists, listicles, step-by-step tutorials, and Instagram pictorials in your content calendar.

You might expect that Generation Z—having grown up surrounded by technology— might ignore ads by nature. But that is not the case. 55 percent of Generation Z self-report that they will pay attention to ads if they are humorous, 45 percent say they will pay attention if the ads have great music.[135]

Generation Z has a unique, dry sense of humor. They thrive on self-deprecating snaps and memes, and videos that make them seem idiosyncratic and one-of-a-kind. While Millennials avoid posting anything that makes them seem outside the social norm, Generation Z is constantly trying to differentiate their personal brands. Brands that bake pithy, smart humor and self-deprecation into their content will likely win over Generation Z. However, if this does not come naturally, do not force it. No brand wants to come across as the grandparent that hops on Snapchat trying to be "high-key" cool.

Gen Z is changing up previous conceptions about social media.

Generation Z's spending power will easily eclipse that of the millennial generation. But marketers trying to make Gen Z grab their wallets can't default to the marketing tactics that worked with Millennials. This notoriously particular generation isn't interested in

Facebook ads littered with OMGs and LOLs. Marketers must meet Gen Z consumers on their social channels at the right times and with campaigns the generation cares about, in the formats they need them.[136]

ASK YOURSELF...

- Do I have enough content? Is it in the right places?

- How organized is my content on YouTube and Instagram?

- What categories should we create in Instagram story highlights?

- How will you humor your customers?

- What research do I need?

- What research can I pull from already?

- What is the first step?

- What is this dependent on?

- What can I do today to move this forward?

RULE #6: BE THE HUSTLE

A recession mindset has led to some serious hustle among Generation Z. This generation spends time envisioning being at the top of their career then takes immediate action to start working towards their goals. Marketers will do well to align their brand with values of hard work, education, and stories of inspiring entrepreneurs, high-profile leaders, or extreme athletes who have succeeded by using your product or service.

Red Bull is an example of a brand doing original content creation that taps into this mindset. They do an unbelievable job producing their video series, and its 8 million YouTube subscribers seem to agree! Instead of showing products, it entertains and engages Generation Z consumers with beautifully-produced video that captures attention, keeps them watching, and develops a relationship between brand and customer. Instead of sponsoring an influencer to showcase their drink, they have chosen to go bigger: original content with larger-than-life production and themes. This creative aligns with the carefully crafted and curated lifestyle brand they want to portray.

Here is an example of one of the videos created by Red Bull for this audience: https://www.youtube.com/watch?time_continue=59&v=0y04vdZvmag

In this video, a BMX rider jumps out of a helicopter while on his bike onto the rooftop of a famous Dubai hotel. If that is not enough action to engage an active 20-something, I don't know what is. This content single-mindedly focuses on the enjoyment of the viewer, and not once utters the benefits of Red Bull. Tapping into the interests that the company knows will pique its audience's attention, Red Bull sells its brand without pushing its product. In turn, they grow an audience that will start to associate Red Bull with thrilling content.

By publishing videos, blog posts, landing pages, and more at the same professional production level, Red Bull successfully aligns its brand with values of focus, precision, and being at the top of your game. To a Generation Z youth, that might mean BMX, sure, but it might also mean starting a business, climbing the corporate ladder, finishing school, or any other type of forward-looking career trajectory.

Marketers, whatever your product or service, whatever your industry, one thing is certain: be clear and focused in your message, and connect it to the advancement of your Generation Z customers.

Alongside their career growth concerns, Generation Z thinks about building wealth and saving money every day. Encourage the hustle by giving them content around these two areas. Many brands avoid the topic of money because they think it does not fit with their brand or it might feel awkward. Even if your brand is not in the financial services sphere, you can still implement this strategy.

For example, imagine if Spotify created a video campaign with niche musicians talking about saving money, and also sharing their backstories from before they made it. They could do a savings playlist and create a partnership with a cool financial brand like Mint to implement some sort of co-branded competition: "Are you saving for something big? Tell us how you saved money this week." Coupled with a hashtag nad competition for $500, something like this could gain a lot of traction. While this is just a hypothetical example, the idea is clear: talk about money because your customers are thinking about it anyway. A brand doing this will catch their attention. Encourage the hustle and forward-looking focus with Instagram posts, games, and competitions with and brand-aware hashtags. Involve personalities and slice-of-life stories.

This hard-working generation has been called frugal, but they will spend money if they believe the value is high enough—up to half their income, in fact. So focus on the outcomes: demonstrate and communicate for them the full breath of value compared to price. What will they ultimately get out of it, even if the value is derived further down the road? Include real customer stories on Instagram or Snapchat.

Whether B2C or B2B, one thing you can do to get storytelling-type content that resonates with Generation Z is to tap into successful entrepreneurs: This generation ardently respects and admires entrepreneurs. Showcase stories of entrepreneurs who have used your product or endorsed your brand—or even your own founder's startup story. Remember, for this generation, interesting content beats fresh content. Even if it's not today's news, as long as it ties into your brand and works with your overarching marketing strategy, it will likely boost engagement with a Generation Z audience.

Another tactic to try that is especially effective for B2B is to partner with co-working spaces. As Generation Z enters the workforce, we are seeing an explosion in co-working spaces because of the sheer number of freelancers, startups, and virtual working. Partner with and advertise in trendy co-working spaces. Especially if you are B2B, running workshops or sponsoring events in these types of spaces could be a good play and would encourage in-person events which would likely foster a stronger of a relationship than through social media alone.

As hard-working doers, they say yes to a lot. Anything your brand can do to help with their schedule chaos would be seen as a big relief. There is no good way for Generation Z to keep track of all the things they have to do. Anything you can do to simplify their time tracking or to-do list would ease some pressure. For instance, if you are marketing an event, make sure it has an "Add to Calendar" button. For appointments, create automatic email and/or text message reminders. Since we started doing this for Generation Z research participants we scheduled through Calendly, we saw a remarkable drop in our no-shows as well. Enable re-scheduling online so that they can do it themselves 24/7 without having to call you.

Along with this time obsession comes a generation obsessed with hacks. Can your marketing content teach people to do something in a clever, resourceful way? Call it a "hack" and add it to your marketing, social media, or content strategy. This is not just for B2C either. B2B Marketers: for you it might just be as simple as putting the word "hack" in your content titles. A couple of years ago, I spoke at 12 conferences in 12 months, many of them in the Digital Summit / Internet Summit series where it was the same conference with the same type of audience, just in a different city. I gave the same presentation at a number of conferences, and when I did nothing but change the name of my conference presentation from "Lean 'N Mean UX" to "UX Hacks to Build Better Products, Faster", I saw a huge increase in people who chose to come to my conference track. The content was the same. The session description was the same. The speaker was the same. All that changed was the title. Now, my talk was mostly to digital marketing Millennials. Imagine if they were Gen Z! You can do this too, at conferences, yes, but also in the titles of videos, social media posts, eBooks, or any other content your brand is creating and distributing.

ASK YOURSELF...

- How can I incorporate people at the top of their games to my brand and in my content?
- How can I talk about growing wealth or saving?
- Which brands can I partner with?
- What can I do today to move this forward?
- How can my brand bring relief to their chaotic lives?
- How can I feature hacks in my content?

RULE #7: STAND FOR SOMETHING

Corporate Social Responsibility is by no means a Millennial fad. Social impact is very important to Generation Z as well, who will respect your brand more if it inspires and reminds them to live an altruistic life.

While this is a no-brainer for Fortune 500 companies, many mid-sized or small companies wonder if the benefits are worth it. Where Generation Z is involved, the answer is categorically YES. The dollar amount is less important than the fact that your company stands for something. It is always a positive story when people are helping others, even if your financial contribution is less than large companies, you can still benefit from the exposure.

Be strategic with the cause(s) you support. Either choose a cause that is in some way related to your line of business (e.g., WW choosing childhood obesity as their social focus) or a cause that is close to home for your employees.

When selling a B2C product, anytime you can incorporate donation as a part of the sale, Generation Z will buy more. That is one of the many reasons why Warby Parker is selling its hipster glasses to the youth in such big numbers. Creative forms of social impact can be especially eye-catching for the youth market. Take New Belgium Brewing Company for instance, who strives to be a sustainable business by using solar panels to power their bottling plant, utilizing an anaerobic digester to convert wastewater into energy, and encouraging their employees to bike around the brewery.

Following in the footsteps of B2C companies, B2B brands are increasingly turning to causes in an effort to differentiate their brands and strengthen loyalty among young customers. For B2B, if your prospects are local businesses, consider focusing on local impact to get the best results. If you are looking to sell to large enterprises, align with the charities they support; philanthropy events are an ideal way to help you network and generate new leads.

In recent years, companies have become increasingly political with their causes. However, given the still forming political beliefs that Generation Z embodies, this a risky choice. Generation Z is both fiscally conservative and socially liberal. Any one-sided cause your brand decides to get behind—even if it seems like it would be popular to a young crowd (e.g., supporting free college tuition)—could isolate large groups of your potential audience.

In order for your company to receive a big impact, you must get the word out about the good you are doing. This is no time to be humble, but you also need to be authentic. Generation Z cares about social issues, and they are more likely to engage with brands that care about those same issues. But they will know if you are not the real deal. Your corporate social responsibility needs to be based on something the brand actually believes in, not just something you say or do to look good. Share content related to social impact stories on your Instagram feed or create YouTube videos to show how you have made an impact, and why it matters to you and your brand. This is one of the key ways to build brand loyalty with Generation Z. Tell your customers and/or leads about your efforts and invite them to join in the conversation and the cause.

In addition to raising brand awareness, having a strong corporate social responsibility plan that engages employees may boost morale of existing employees and differentiate you when attempting to attract top talent. Ensure that the charity you choose resonates with your employees. Many organizations choose a matching program so employees can control where the dollars are spent. But to communicate what your brand stands for in the best way, focus your efforts with singular intention. The KPMG Foundation, for example, has gained traction by consistently sticking to its objective to support educational and social projects for the disadvantaged and underprivileged. Many of these projects are led by employees at the firm.

So show Generation Z what your brand stands for, and educate them on the cause to foster feel-good learning, and give them opportunities to participate in the conversation to encourage a personal stake and increased loyalty.

Practicing corporate responsibility does something more for the brand that marketers (especially in the era of fast-moving social media) should pay attention to: it serves as a form of "reputation insurance" against any negative publicity your company may get. It builds up a "reservoir of goodwill" that protects firms from sustaining long-term damage following adverse events, and helps them recover more quickly.[137]

Social marketing is in. Couple this with in-person event marketing and you will have a far bigger impact on teens. Generation Z expects to interact and co-create with your brand, and there is an opportunity for in-person event marketing that is passing many marketers by. Today's marketers keep blasting on social media, but today's teens are growing weary of the superficiality and are craving connection. They associate positive feelings with in-person events, especially those that are socially driven. For a social-conscious brand, it seems like a no-brainer to sponsor an event related to social change, show up in person, and start to develop a real relationship between your brand and customers. They are constantly bombarded by ads on their phone, and what they need is something altogether different: something that gets them off their phones and makes them feel a little less lonely in the world.

An example of a campaign that combines a social cause with an in-person event was the #WalkUpNotOut movement after the tragic high school shooting in Parkland, Florida that urged high school students to reach out to students perceived as socially isolated. No matter your position on gun control, shifting student focus to community and kindness transcends politics. This event tapped into local sentiment, blew up on social media, and encouraged face-to-face interaction. At a time when 1 in 5 Americans reports having meaningful in-person encounters less than once a week, this is the type of powerful event that will resonate and be remembered.

Choose a cause related to your brand, and make sure Generation Z knows what your brand stands for. Brands that make a positive contribution to society are more likely to appeal to young buyers. Focus your marketing messages on helping people, and socially-conscious Generation Z will respond.

ASK YOURSELF...

- What does my brand stand for?

- What should my brand stand for?

- If we were to pick one cause, what would it be?

- How does that cause relate to my industry or employees?

- What research do I need?

- What can I do today to move this forward?

RULE #8: CREATE SEAMLESS, PERSONALIZED EXPERIENCES

To connect with Generation Z, technology must be invisible. This generation ricochets between digital touchpoints like a pinball machine. Desktop website. Mobile app. Mobile website. Talk to a smart speaker. Text customer service. Call customer service. Press 1, 2, 1, 2, 1, 2, 0, 0, 0, 0, 0 and finally drop the call with customer service. Twitter for customer service. Tablet website. Tablet app. Smart speaker with screen. Walk into retail store. Snapchat while in store. Self-pay kiosk. Mobile app. Mobile site. Brand page on Instagram… the list goes on.

Despite this turbulent behavior, if Generation Z notices even the slightest slowdown or inconvenience—even if it was due to their device switching—it is all over and any loyalty you had built up will be gone in an instant. With this generation, perfectly executed, seamless transitions are a must. Of course, everything needs to work flawlessly on mobile as well, preferably in an app over a mobile website.

If Generation Z notices the technology, you are doing something wrong.

Generation Z has grown up with constant connection. This has fundamentally changed their perception of convenience, and they expect a lot more from you. Everything is about speed, and time is directly linked to customer experience. While they may be more demanding, compared to other generations, they are actually willing to pay for convenience. How Generation Z expects products and services to be delivered creates new opportunities for marketers to explore various channels. Same-day delivery and mobile self-checkouts in stores may be the key to loyalty for this generation.

Experiment with new ways to capture loyalty, as today brand loyalty is harder than ever to earn. Do not bother with coupons. The following elements trump traditional loyalty programs for Generation Z: (1) superior mobile experiences; (3) feel-good branding; (4) sheer speed of checkout and delivery; (5) family/friend recommendations. Focus on enhancing one or all of these for a shot at capturing some elusive Generation Z loyalty.

Personalization is key to not being ignored by Generation Z. However, from my own research on customer delight, for youth, personalization is not delightful; it is *expected*. In order to make this happen, you have to be fully enthralled with giving your customers precisely what they need, when they need it. While Generation Z is a more cautious group when it comes to sharing content publicly, they do not hesitate to give out their personal information to a profile in exchange for the promise of a more cultivated experience. That makes this generation perfect for account-based marketing, a practice that is quickly gaining steam within B2B. With more complete personal information entered by these customers, your company will be able to do more predictive analytics, segment more effectively, strategically create products and content that align to their needs, at just the right times. Conduct ongoing research to find out who they are, what segments you want to personalize for, and then do it.

ASK YOURSELF...

- How much friction occurs in our customer experiences?
- What is the ultimate goal?
- What does success look like?
- What has stopped you in the past?
- What research do I need?
- What research can I pull from already?
- What is the first step?
- What is this dependent on?
- What can I do today to move this forward?

RULE #9: SUPPORT BUYING IN YOUR CUSTOMER'S RESEARCH PHASE

As a digital marketer, you have inevitably seen a funnel at some point that breaks down the buyer's journey into key phases: awareness; interest; research; purchase; post-purchase; re-purchase. Through each one of these phases, we as marketers have unique opportunities to support Generation Z in their buying decisions.

We have covered a lot about generating awareness and sparking interest in this book. Now we get to talk about the research phase, and how marketers can support buying decisions at this time. Generation Z demands more value for their money, and is willing to spend time conducting voluminous research on any potential purchase. As marketers, we can help them along in this endeavor in a few key ways.

First, we can provide them with easily scannable details they need in quick visual formats—for instance, a list of the services or features you offer and how top competitors stack up. Just make sure this type of matrix is able to be readily viewed on mobile, as Generation Z is twice as likely to convert on mobile over any other demographic.[138]

What is even better though is having details across a range of pages and in a number of places. The more information on various pages the better, as Generation Z views 62 percent more pages while researching than any other generation, in half the time![139] This generation feels guilty if they do not do enough research (to get the most value for their money), so they are compelled to go from page to page, looking at all the details, trying to feel confident that they are making an informed purchase decision.

If you are selling a product, focus on reviews in a big way. While Millennials tend to look at just the 5 star and 1 star reviews, Generation Z reads all reviews. As a brand, get involved. Respond to negative reviews on Amazon and Yelp as long as they are reasonable, and try to resolve any issues or complaints with standout customer service. Oftentimes, good customer service is enough to compel someone to modify a review.

For luxury items (ones that young 20-somethings can afford once they start working), run mid-week campaigns. This is the time when young consumers tend to make more impulse purchases. It is mostly because they are by themselves, working and commuting and going to the gym. They hang out with friends more on the weekends; on the weeknights they are typically alone. And if they are not gaming, they are probably browsing, possibly scanning eyes over your product or service.

Whatever you do, be up-front about the total price. Do not charge extra for shipping. Amazon changed the name of the game on that one. All-inclusive is best.

What is fascinating to me about this stage is that we tend to see much more sharing pre-purchase than post-purchase, which is not typically when brands are encouraging people to share. Most brands tend to focus on sharing CTAs after a purchase. But to younger consumers, this feels like bragging. To encourage Generation Z to share purchases, remind them during the research stage instead of post-purchase. Sharing is extremely important for B2B and B2C brands alike. 68 percent of Generation Z consumers said they would refer a product to a friend, and 41 percent said they would do so for an incentive. Seeing how users are more influenced by friend/family recommendations than anything else (and how they influence brand loyalty more than anything else), this seems like a good spot to place your focus.

During the research stage, unlike Millennials, Generation Z tends to visit stores in-person for more tactile browsing. Keep in mind, they do have their phones glued to them and are constantly snapping photos during these trips. Knowing this, marketers can add ways to connect and engage with the brand while on your phone in a store. For example, during Adidas' "Here to Create" campaign, local Snapchat filters encouraged a whopping 18 percent increase in new visitors to Adidas stores.

Snapchat filters were used to spark creativity, engage youth, and get these audiences to walk into stores in big numbers.[140]

ASK YOURSELF...

- How do my customers find me?

- What research do they do pre-purchase?

- What research is required for re-ordering?

- Where in the research stage can I encourage sharing?

- What would make my pricing more transparent?

- What is this all dependent on?

- What can I do today to move this forward?

RULE #10: MANUFACTURE DELIGHT WITHIN THE JOURNEY

When was the last time you were truly delighted by a product or service?

Go ahead, think about it. It's hard, right? Past marketers have described delight as being "pleasure" above functionality: more than reliability and usability, that something extra that brings an added degree of pleasure to a customer. But that seems so flat. Just because something pleases you doesn't mean it really delights you. I mean, if it were that easy, why aren't more products or services... well, delightful?

When we look at what really causes someone to be truly delighted, it is different (and substantially more complex) than what causes them to be simply pleased. There is a range of emotions that goes into the sense of delight. It is never just satisfaction or pleasure. I conducted a study with 250 people where I asked that simple question I just referenced: When was the last time you were truly delighted by a product, service, or experience?

What I found: while 24 percent of people equated delight with pleasure, 58 percent talked about surprise and 82 percent talked about relief.

One 20-something remarked, "I purchased a taco at a surfside taco stand and was thrilled. I've had a lot of so-so tacos in the past. This taco had so much flavor."

Another explained, "Wearing my new hiking boots for the first time. I used to hike in sneakers. Excited to have a real pair of hiking boots, and excited to [explore] the outdoors."

This even extends more universally, to older generations as well. One parent of a Generation Z child told me, "Amazon Fresh offered a 20-pound turkey for just 99 cents before Thanksgiving! It was an unexpected bonus and totally thrilled me. Saved me time and money. What a relief around the holidays."

So what did you notice in these stories? Whether it was a so-so taco, hiking in sneakers, or cooking thanksgiving dinner, there was some sort of past anxiety, coupled with relief, and that created delight. What kind of relief? 25 percent described time savings, 21 percent described customer service, and 11 percent described a personalized experience. What's more, over 60 percent of the participants in our study who talked about relief also described surprise. Given this, we can create a formula for you to manufacture delight for your brand, again and again:

DELIGHT = RELIEF + SURPRISE

You got it: that elusive feeling of delight can actually be re-created time and again for your customers by just adding unexpected surprises that offer relief: saving time, money, or offering something that seems personal to that customer.

How do we know this works with Generation Z? Because in a recent study, 83 percent are more loyal to brands that offer value-added rewards and surprises. Not to mention that 82 percent of those who get a surprise reward spend it immediately, on whatever special promotion or offer is included with it.[141] Prepaid gift cards seem to be the highest-converting reward, with customers typically spending more than is on the gift card. Generation Z is twice as likely to prefer a gift card over either a check or PayPal loyalty incentive.[142]

"Brands are at a crossroads with the shifting loyalty of Generation Z and young Millennials, requiring a fresh approach to engaging this next generation of buyers," said Rodney Mason, Swift's Chief Revenue Officer. "As brands develop new strategies, incentives and referral programs using prepaid cards will become more crucial to recruit, retain and grow their customer base by appealing to buyer's wallets and communities."

ASK YOURSELF...

- Do I have personas for my key target audiences?

- Do I have a map for these audiences' journeys?

- Am I able to pinpoint the key points of anxiety throughout their journeys?

- For each point of anxiety, what could I do to provide my customer relief? Surprise? Both?

- What could I do to save my customer time?

- At what points would added customer service make things feel easier for my customer?

- How can I personalize the experience for each of my target customers?

RULE #11: RESEARCH YOUR SPECIFIC CUSTOMERS

You now know the top trends in terms of digital usage, social media behavior, and buying decisions across this new generation. Do not be alarmed if many of them seem surprising; Generation Z thinks and acts so differently compared to past generations that many of these trends are not immediately intuitive to the marketer.

Of course, to provide your customers with the most targeted approach, you will need to continue your research. You will want to know specifically what makes your customers tick. You will want to know what differentiators cause them to choose you, and which cause them to choose a competitor. You will want to know what inspires them so you can create more targeted content and campaigns. You will want to know what skills they want or need to learn so you can provide them. You will want to know related interests and personalities they follow so you can more effectively cut through the noise and capture attention. You will want to know what specifically flips the switch and motivates them to move past the research stage into a purchase so you can catapult them there faster.

There is always more to learn, more to know. And since you have almost made it to the end of the book, I know that you are hungry for it. You won't have to spend your valuable research time and dollars re-creating the wheel because you have learned the basic trends for this generation. Additionally, knowing more about Generation Z, you can can make better-informed hypotheses that guide the path to the creation of more targeted customer research studies.

On top of this you now know a research group you can call for help planning or conducting future customer research studies for you: a group that truly knows about Generation Z because we have literally written the book on it. #ShamlessPlug

It's easy to know what's not working. It's harder to find out why—and what to do about it. Your research will need to get into the minds of your specific customers and deliver fresh, new psychological insights that drive strategic decisions.

The big-picture goal of any deep customer research is to peel back the layers to uncover the "why" behind your customers' behaviors. This empowers you to be confident in the fact that you are offering the right products and services for the right reasons.

In conducting hundreds of research projects over the past 15 years, there are 3 common reasons companies wish to conduct marketing research or customer research:

1. Spot new opportunities
2. Ensure a prototype or product works for customers or potential customers
3. Measure and optimize customer experience over time

If your goal is to spot new opportunities for your business or brand, you need to be confident in what your customers (and potential customers) really need, not just what they say they need. As Henry Ford famously noted, "If I had asked people what they wanted, they would have said faster horses." Often customers cannot envision or articulate what they need because they do not spend their days (as you do!) brainstorming and obsessing about all possible opportunities to make their experience with you better.

This is where design thinking and service design comes into play, with help from a few of these favored psychographic research techniques:

- Contextual Interviews
- Ethnography
- Mobile Diary Studies
- Journey Mapping
- Visioning & Innovation Workshops

If you have a product that you think is close to being market-ready, you will want to find out how your customers or potential customers will react. If your goal is a new product or a new extension of a product, you can readily test sketches, prototypes, or developed products. At any point along the way, you should be able to quickly find out if you are ready for launch and prevent a rollout disaster by verifying the viability of your product.

For this scenario, you may wish to collect your research using these methods:

- Usability Testing
- Agile/Lean Testing
- Intercept Interviews & Guerrilla Testing
- Rapid Prototyping
- A/B Testing
- Expert Reviews

The third common goal companies have is to measure over time and optimize their existing customer experience. With this goal, you will want to know for sure which updates matter the most to your customers to ensure that your Key Performance Indicators (KPIs) are being met. In this scenario, your best bet for research approaches may be:

- Quantitative Research
- Ongoing Experience Measurement
- Competitor Ranking
- Content & Messaging Evaluations
- Eye-tracking & Biometric Studies

Once you understand your goal, list out all the questions that you need to answer. This step helps you to clearly articulate what you want to know about your customers that you do not know already. Writing what you want to know in the form of questions helps you to hone your focus and write a research plan to tackle very specific questions. After you have completed your research, this also helps you to double check that you are able to confidently answer each question, to measure the success of your study.

Once you have these questions drafted, you may find it helpful to look at the data you have (past research, analytics, etc.) and identify gaps between the data you have and the answers you need. I encourage this because you should be striving to get very specific research insights.

Leveraging past research is a good starting point to help you go deeper and answer the tough questions.

For B2C companies, perhaps you want to know the precise trigger that moves a potential customer from the research stage to a buying stage—and specifically what elements of your interface move the needle. Past journey mapping or persona research might kickstart this process, and let your research team more quickly move to that answer.

For B2B companies, you may want to know what causes repeat buyers to even think about switching to a competitor. Perhaps you have analytics that narrow it down to a specific page where they drop out of a funnel. This gives you a jumping off point to really dig into what is going on in this step of their journey.

With a clear plan of action, creating a specific research script, conducting targeted research, and interpreting results become far more streamlined and on-point.

ASK YOURSELF...

- What is the big-picture goal: identify market opportunities, launch the right product, or optimize an existing customer experience?

- What do I want to know about my customer that I currently do not know?

- What questions about my customer would help me more effectively capture attention, educate consumers, or boost conversions?

- Which questions are of highest priority to me and my stakeholders?

- What gaps exist between my existing research and what I want to know?

- What research methods might be best for this study, based on my goal?

- Do I have enough information to create a research plan?

- Are my stakeholders aligned?

- When do I need the research by?

- What is my budget?

- Should I do the research in-house or outsource to a customer research studio?

Need help articulating your goals, or creating your research plan, or conducting research? Visit www.sarahweise.com or email hello@sarahweise.com

IN CLOSING

Marketing is all about influencing behavior, right? Ha. Forget trying to influence Generation Z; Generation Z will influence you. How do I know? Because they have already done it. Like no other generation before them, Generation Z and Millennials have actively assimilated previous generations into their culture. People of all ages are snapping selfies and responding with emojis over text, and many are even jumping on the Snapchat bandwagon. The over-65 crowd is more likely than any other generation to report that it is "always appropriate" to send emojis in a work setting to a direct manager, peer, or subordinate.[143] Considered mainstays of modern culture, new behaviors have rippled through the generations. People of all ages want to know what's top-of-mind on social media, and look to younger generations for cues on how to use and leverage technology. Generation Z is influencing how we live and work, far more than you might think.

Generation Z is reshaping the social media landscape, and marketers need to adapt their strategies if they have any chance of tapping into the big opportunities that lie ahead with this generation of consumers. By following the blueprint I have laid out in *InstaBrain*—these new rules of marketing—you can restructure your marketing strategy with confidence: capturing more attention, educating more customers, and closing more sales. You will also be able to move beyond the basics in your research and learn in more detail what works for your specific customers.

In the coming years, Generation Z will make their mark. The unique way they work, sell, buy, communicate, and ultimately...lead is totally different than previous generations. The leaders who understand the values, expectations and behaviors of Generation Z will be better positioned for next generation success, and ultimately, win.

I hope that this book has helped you to understand this new and incredibly important wave of consumers, and gain some fresh, creative ideas about how to change your marketing strategy or what types of research you may need going forward.

Thank you for reading!

Sarah

. . . .

www.sarahweise.com
hello@sarahweise.com
LinkedIn: linkedin.com/in/sarahweise
Twitter: @weisesarah
Instagram: @sarahvweise

HAVE SARAH WEISE SPEAK TO YOUR TEAM!

"A moment's insight is sometimes worth a life's experience."

- Oliver Wendell Holmes Jr.

Sarah will inspire your company or team to tap into what we know about Generation Z to capture attention, educate consumers, and boost sales.

Most companies spend a considerable amount of time, effort, and money building products and marketing them. Yet there almost always remains a gap between the customer's expectations and what is actually delivered. Sarah can teach your team how to shrink this gap: how to leverage your customer research—and what we already know about Generation Z—to create a knockout strategy that you can start applying right away.

Sarah's engaging and interactive sessions range from a one-hour keynote to a one-day workshop, and offer fresh insight into what it takes to understand *your* customers and implement a new strategy to connect with them.

> ## To Hire Sarah To Speak To Your Team:
> www.sarahweise.com
> press@sarahweise.com
> 301-541-7699

ENDNOTES

1   Throughout this book, participant names have been changed.

2   Jeremy Finch, "What is Generation Z, and What Does It Want?" Fast Company, May 4, 2015, http://www.fastcompany.com/3045317/what-is-generation-z-and-what-does-it-want.

3   "Activities of Kids and Teens-US," Mintel Reports, November 2013.

4   Calculations by Jeff From and Angie Read based on data from 2015 USDA child expenditures, 2016 US Census data, and 2016 Bureau of Labor Statistics consumer expenditure data. Cited in Fromm, Jeff, and Angie Read. *Marketing to Gen Z the Rules for Reaching This Vast and Very Different Generation of Influencers.* AMACOM, 2018.

5   "World Population Prospects: The 2017 Revision | Multimedia Library - United Nations Department of Economic and Social Affairs." *United Nations,* www.un.org/development/desa/publications/world-population-prospects-the-2017-revision.html.

6   "Q2 2017: Upcoming Reports from GlobalWebIndex." *GlobalWebIndex Blog,* 25 Apr. 2017, blog.globalwebindex.com/trends/upcoming-reports-from-globalwebindex-q2-2017/.

7   Maheshwari, Sapna. "Are You Ready for the Nanoinfluencers?" The New York Times, The New York Times, 11 Nov. 2018, www.nytimes.com/2018/11/11/business/media/nanoinfluencers-instagram-influencers.html.

8   Fromm, Jeff, and Angie Read. *Marketing to Gen Z the Rules for Reaching This Vast and Very Different Generation of Influencers.* AMACOM, 2018.

9   Garvey, Anna. "The Oregon Trail Generation: Life Before and After Mainstream Tech." Social Media Week, 13 Oct. 2015, socialmediaweek.org/blog/2015/04/oregon-trail-generation/.

10   Hipp, Patrick. "Fuck You, I'm Not A Millennial – Patrick Hipp – Medium." Medium.com, Medium, 13 Mar. 2016, medium.com/@thehipp/fuck-you-i-m-not-a-millennial-e92e653ceb39.

11   "Top 15 Merit Badges for Millennial Life Achievements." Crazy Funny Pictures, 12 Jan. 2018, www.eatliver.com/millennials/.

12   Meyer, Zlati. "Avocado Toast Sneakers Are Now a Thing, Thanks to Saucony, Er, Saucamole." USA Today, Gannett Satellite Information Network, 27 Feb. 2019, www.usatoday.com/story/money/2019/02/27/avocado-toast-sneakers-debut-saucony/3003017002/?utm_source=-feedblitz&utm_medium=FeedBlitzRss&utm_campaign=u-satodaycommoney-topstories.

13   Scott, Ryan. Get Ready For Generation Z. 28 Nov. 2016, www.forbes.com/sites/causeintegration/2016/11/28/get-ready-for-generation-z/#2611904c2204.

14   KIDS COUNT Data Book. Annie E. Casey Foundation, 2018, www.aecf.org/resources/2018-kids-count-data-book/.

15   "Cross-Cultural Gen Z." Futurecasting Hispanic Millennials and the New "Hispanic Initiative" | Sensis, www.sensisagency.com/blog/20160623/cross-cultural-gen-z.

16   "Step Aside Millennials: Gen Z Has Arrived." *Ideas In Digital (iid)*, 28 Dec. 2018, iid.co/step-aside-Millennials-gen-z-has-arrived/.

17   Sorrel, Charlie. "The Nuclear Family Is Still The Majority Of U.S. Households–Just Barely." Fast Company, Fast Company, 26 July 2016, www.fastcompany.com/3062162/the-nuclear-family-is-still-the-majority-of-us-households-just-barely.

18   Krogstad, Jens Manuel. "5 Facts about the Modern American Family." Pew Research Center, 30 Apr. 2014, www.pewresearch.org/fact-tank/2014/04/30/5-facts-about-the-modern-american-family/.

19   White, John. "Learn Why Top Gen Zers Are Skipping School to Become Entrepreneurs." *Inc.com*, Inc., 11 Sept. 2017, www.inc.com/john-white/learn-why-top-gen-zers-are-skipping-school-to-beco.html.

20   Sorrel, Charlie. "The Nuclear Family Is Still The Majority Of U.S. Households–Just Barely." Fast Company, Fast Company, 26 July 2016, www.fastcompany.com/3062162/the-nuclear-family-is-still-the-majority-of-us-households-just-barely.

21   "Multiracial Children," American Academy of Child & Adolescent Psychiatry, April 2016. https://www.aacap.org/aacap/families_and_youth/facts_for_families/fff-guide/Multiracial-Children-071.aspx

22   Carrasco, Mario. "3 Reasons Why Gen Z Will Disrupt Multicultural Marketing Models," MediaPost, Aug 4, 2016. https://www.mediapost.com/publications/article/280961/3-reasons-gen-z-will-disrupt-multicultural-marketi.html

23   Parker, Kim, et al. "Generation Z Looks a Lot Like Millennials on Key Social and Political Issues." *Pew Research Center's Social & Demographic Trends Project*, Pew Research Center's Social & Demographic Trends Project, 18 Jan. 2019, www.pewsocialtrends.org/2019/01/17/generation-z-looks-a-lot-like-millennials-on-key-social-and-political-issues/.

24   Fromm, Jeff, and Angie Read. *Marketing to Gen Z the Rules for Reaching This Vast and Very Different Generation of Influencers.* AMACOM, 2018.

25   "Step Aside Millennials: Gen Z Has Arrived." *Ideas In Digital (iid)*, 28 Dec. 2018, iid.co/step-aside-millennials-gen-z-has-arrived/.

26   "Attention Span Statistics." *Statistic Brain*, 9 July 2018, www.statisticbrain.com/attention-span-statistics/.

27   Ibid.

28   "Mark Zuckerberg Promises to Improve Facebook Privacy. Sound Familiar?" *Fortune,* fortune.com/2019/03/06/ mark-zuckerberg-improve-privacy-facebook/.

29   Molina, Brett. "Does Your Kid Have a 'Finsta' Account? Why It's a Big Deal." USA Today, Gannett Satellite Information Network, 20 Oct. 2017, www.usatoday.com/story/tech/talkingtech/2017/10/20/ does-your-kid-have-finsta-account-why-its-big-deal/783424001/.

30   Ward, Adrian F, et al. Brain Drain: The Mere Presence of One's Own Smartphone Reduces Available Cognitive Capacity. *Journal of the Association of Consumer Research*, 3 Apr. 2017, www.journals. uchicago.edu/doi/abs/10.1086/691462.

31   "Step Aside Millennials: Gen Z Has Arrived." *Ideas In Digital (iid)*, 28 Dec. 2018, iid.co/step-aside-millennials-gen-z-has-arrived/.

32   Looper, Christian de, and Christian de Looper. "82 Percent of U.S. Teens Use an IPhone -- And It's Growing." Digital Trends, Digital Trends, 10 Apr. 2018, www.digitaltrends.com/mobile/ iphone-use-teens-2018/.

33   "How to Connect to Gen Z, the Post-Digital Generation." *Millennial Marketing*, www.millennialmarketing.com/2018/03/ how-to-connect-to-gen-z-the-post-digital-generation/.

34   "Step Aside Millennials: Gen Z Has Arrived." *Ideas In Digital (iid)*, 28 Dec. 2018, iid.co/step-aside-millennials-gen-z-has-arrived/.

35   Statistic Brain. "Attention Span Statistics." *Statistic Brain*, 9 July 2018, www.statisticbrain.com/attention-span-statistics/.

36   "The Future of Digital Communication Study." *SendGrid*, go.send-grid.com/Future-of-Digital-Communication-Study.html.

37   Ibid.

38   Sloane, Garett. "Facebook: Fast-Scrolling Millennials Consume Ads 2.5 Times Faster." *Digiday*, 30 Sept. 2015, digiday.com/ media/advertisingweek2015-facebook-finds-that-fast-scrollin g-millennials-consume-ads-2-5-times-faster/.

39   "Gen Z Prefer Fun Content Over Friends on Social."
      GlobalWebIndex Blog, 28 Feb. 2018, blog.globalwebindex.com/
      chart-of-the-day/gen-z-social/.

40   Lorenz, Taylor. "Generation Z Is Already Bored by the Internet."
      The Daily Beast, The Daily Beast Company, 3 Apr. 2018, www.
      thedailybeast.com/generation-z-is-already-bored-by-the-internet.

41   Ibid

42   Lorenz, Taylor. "Generation Z Is Already Bored by the Internet."
      The Daily Beast, The Daily Beast Company, 3 Apr. 2018, www.
      thedailybeast.com/generation-z-is-already-bored-by-the-internet.

43   Joyce, Alita, and Jakob Nielsen. "Teenager's UX: Designing
      for Teens." *Nielsen Norman Group*, www.nngroup.com/articles/
      usability-of-websites-for-teenagers/. 17 March 2019.

44   "Gen Z Prefer Fun Content Over Friends on Social."
      GlobalWebIndex Blog, 28 Feb. 2018, blog.globalwebindex.com/
      chart-of-the-day/gen-z-social/.

45   "Gen Z Prefer Fun Content Over Friends on Social."
      GlobalWebIndex Blog, 28 Feb. 2018, blog.globalwebindex.com/
      chart-of-the-day/gen-z-social/.

46   "Why Influencer Marketing Works for Generation Z." *We Are Social
      UK - Global Socially-Led Creative Agency*, 6 July 2017, wearesocial.
      com/uk/blog/2017/05/influencer-marketing-works-generation-z.

47   "Gen Z Engaging with 10 Hours of Online Content a Day."
      Marketing Tech News, www.marketingtechnews.net/news/2018/
      feb/09/gen-z-engaging-10-hours-online-content-day/.

48   Parker, Ashley. "Inside Kim Kardashian And Kanye West's $30
      Million NYC Airbnb." *Yahoo! News*, Yahoo!, 21 Sept. 2016, www.
      yahoo.com/news/inside-kim-kardashian-kanye-wests-120401385.
      html.

49   "This Is How Many Americans Use Their Phones On The Toilet [Infographic]." *Daily Infographic*, 29 Oct. 2017, www.dailyinfographic.com/how-many-americans-use-phones-on-toilet.

50   Donovan, Jay, and Jay Donovan. "The Average Age for a Child Getting Their First Smartphone Is Now 10.3 Years." *TechCrunch*, 19 May 2016, techcrunch.com/2016/05/19/the-average-age-for-a-child-getting-their-first-smartphone-is-now-10-3-years/.

51   "Sleep Loss In Teens Linked To Social Media." 17 Jan 2017, www.mediapost.com/publications/article/293065/sleep-loss-in-teens-linked-to-social-media.html.

52   Rose, Sarah. "Sleep Loss in Teens Linked to Social Media." *KNect365*, 15 Feb. 2017, knect365.com/insights/article/27306128-9b12-4957-a20e-af903089aaa8/sleep-loss-in-teens-linked-to-social-media.

53   "Sleep Loss In Teens Linked To Social Media." 17 Jan 2017, www.mediapost.com/publications/article/293065/sleep-loss-in-teens-linked-to-social-media.html.

54   Perrin, Andrew. "5 Facts about Americans and Video Games." *Pew Research Center*, 17 Sept. 2018, www.pewresearch.org/fact-tank/2018/09/17/5-facts-about-americans-and-video-games/.

55   Jeremy Finch, "What is Generation Z, and What Does It Want?" *Fast Company*, May 4, 2015, http://www.fastcompany.com/3045317/what-is-generation-z-and-what-does-it-want.

56   Calculations by Jeff From and Angie Read based on data from 2015 USDA child expenditures, 2016 US Census data, and 2016 Bureau of Labor Statistics consumer expenditure data.

57   Bacon, Jonathan, et al. "Behaviour v Demographics: Why the Term 'Millennial' Is Useless." *Marketing Week*, 20 Sept. 2017, www.marketingweek.com/2016/09/14/behaviour-versus-demographics-why-the-term-millennial-is-useless/#.V9kYPw2SASg.

58   Cassandra report "The Monetization Generation"

59   "Is 'Gen Z' Equipped to Finance Retirement?" *Asppa.org*, 3
      Nov. 2017, www.asppa.org/news-resources/browse-topics/'gen-z
      '-equipped-finance-retirement.

60   "Beyond Millennials: The Next Generation of Learners." *Pearson.*
      Aug 2018. https://www.pearson.com/content/dam/one-dot-com/
      one-dot-com/global/Files/news/news-annoucements/2018/
      The-Next-Generation-of-Learners_final.pdf

61   Jeremy Finch, "What is Generation Z, and What Does It
      Want?" *Fast Company,* May 4, 2015, http://www.fastcompany.
      com/3045317/what-is-generation-z-and-what-does-it-want.

62   "Beyond Millennials: The Next Generation of Learners." *Pearson.*
      Aug 2018. https://www.pearson.com/content/dam/one-dot-com/
      one-dot-com/global/Files/news/news-annoucements/2018/
      The-Next-Generation-of-Learners_final.pdf

63   Fromm, Jeff, and Angie Read. *Marketing to Gen Z the Rules for
      Reaching This Vast and Very Different Generation of Influencers.*
      AMACOM, 2018.

64   White, John. "Learn Why Top Gen Zers Are Skipping School to
      Become Entrepreneurs." *Inc.com*, Inc., 11 Sept. 2017, www.inc.com/
      john-white/learn-why-top-gen-zers-are-skipping-school-to-beco.
      html.

65   "Step Aside Millennials: Gen Z Has Arrived." *Ideas In Digital (iid)*,
      28 Dec. 2018, iid.co/step-aside-millennials-gen-z-has-arrived/.

66   White, John. "Learn Why Top Gen Zers Are Skipping School to
      Become Entrepreneurs." *Inc.com*, Inc., 11 Sept. 2017, www.inc.com/
      john-white/learn-why-top-gen-zers-are-skipping-school-to-beco.
      html.

67   Shanon Insler, "5 Important Money Lessons You Can Learn from
      Generation Z," *Student Loan Hero*, February 14, 2017, https://stu-
      dentloanhero.com/featured/gen-z-5-important-money-lessons

68   "Millennials: Crazy for Coupons." *CSP Daily News*, 19
Sept. 2016, www.cspdailynews.com/technologyservices/
millennials-crazy-coupons.

69   Salpini, Cara. "Gen Z Twice as Influenced by Social Media as by
Deals." *Retail Drive*, 19 Sept. 2017, www.retaildive.com/news/
gen-z-twice-as-influenced-by-social-media-as-by-deals/505274/.

70   Contentsquare. "Generation Z: The Coming of (Shopping) Age."
ContentSquare, go.contentsquare.com/genz.

71   Ibid.

72   Contentsquare. "Generation Z: The Coming of (Shopping) Age."
ContentSquare, go.contentsquare.com/genz.

73   Ibid.

74   Kirkpatrick, David. "Bloomingdale's, Cotton Inc. Roll out
1-Minute Shoppable Fashion Show." *Marketing Dive*, 8 Sept. 2017,
www.marketingdive.com/news/bloomingdales-cotton-inc-roll-out-
1-minute-shoppable-fashion-show/504521/.

75   "10 Facts about Millennials That Every Retailer Should Know."
Buxton, www.buxtonco.com/blog/10-facts-about-millen-
nials-that-every-retailer-should-know.

76   "Gaming: The Key to Gen Z." *The Richards Group*, 21 Nov. 2017,
richards.com/blog/gaming-key-gen-z/.

77   Ibid.

78   Fromm, Jeff, and Angie Read. *Marketing to Gen Z the Rules for
Reaching This Vast and Very Different Generation of Influencers.*
AMACOM, 2018.

79   Caruana, Albert, and Rosella Vassallo. "Children's Perception
of Their Influence over Purchases: the Role of Parental
Communication Patterns." *Journal of Consumer Marketing*, vol. 20,
no. 1, 2003, pp. 55–66., doi:10.1108/07363760310456955.

80 "When It Comes to Gen Z, Forget Everything You Know about Brand Loyalty." *Vision Critical*, www.visioncritical.com/blog/gen-z-brand-loyalty.

81 King, Jennifer. "What Makes Consumers Loyal to Brands?" *EMarketer*, EMarketer, 17 Sept. 2018, www.emarketer.com/content/what-makes-consumers-loyal-to-brands.

82 "When It Comes to Gen Z, Forget Everything You Know about Brand Loyalty." *Vision Critical*, www.visioncritical.com/blog/gen-z-brand-loyalty.

83 Ibid.

84 Jenkins, Ryan. "The Complete Guide to Who Is Generation Z." *Inc.com*, Inc., 25 Sept. 2017, www.inc.com/ryan-jenkins/complete-guide-to-who-is-generation-z.html.

85 Wolverton, Troy. "There's One Big Difference between Spotify's Users and Those on Google, Apple, and Amazon Streaming Products - and It's a Good Sign for Spotify." *Business Insider*, 3 Apr. 2018, www.businessinsider.com/spotify-has-more-loyal-users-than-apple-music-and-pandora-survey-2018-3.

86 Salpini, Cara. "Gen Z Twice as Influenced by Social Media as by Deals." *Retail Dive*, 19 Sept. 2017, www.retaildive.com/news/gen-z-twice-as-influenced-by-social-media-as-by-deals/505274/.

87 "Digital Shopping Features That Would Influence Internet Users in North America to Be Most Loyal to a Brand, Product or Service, by Age, March 2017 (% of Respondents in Each Group)." *EMarketer*, www.emarketer.com/Chart/Digital-Shopping-Features-that-Would-Influence-Internet-Users-North-America-Most-Loyal-Brand-Product-Service-by-Age-March-2017-of-respo/208864.

88 Sweeney, Erica, and Erica Sweeney. "Gen Z Just Wants To Watch Netflix And Get Takeout, And It's Affecting Restaurants." *HuffPost*, 9 July 2018, www.huffpost.com/entry/gen-z-restaurants-takeout_n_5b33a30de4b0b5e692f35f13.

89   Ibid.

90   Smith, Samantha, et al. "Younger, Older Generations Divided in Partisanship and Ideology." *Pew Research Center*, 20 Mar. 2017, www.pewresearch.org/fact-tank/2017/03/20/a-wider-partisan-an d-ideological-gap-between-younger-older-generations/.

91   Parker, Kim, et al. "Generation Z Looks a Lot Like Millennials on Key Social and Political Issues." *Pew Research Center's Social & Demographic Trends Project*, Pew Research Center's Social & Demographic Trends Project, 18 Jan. 2019, www. pewsocialtrends.org/2019/01/17/generation-z-looks-a-lot-lik e-millennials-on-key-social-and-political-issues/.

92   Hassler, Christine. *20 Something Manifesto: Quarter-Lifers Speak out about Who They Are, What They Want, and How to Get It.* New World Library, 2008.

93   Bacon, Jonathan, et al. "Behaviour v Demographics: Why the Term 'Millennial' Is Useless." *Marketing Week*, 20 Sept. 2017, www.marketingweek.com/2016/09/14/ behaviour-versus-demographics-why-the-ter m-millennial-is-useless/#.V9kYPw2SASg.twitter.

94   Stahl, Ashley. "Why Democrats Should Be Losing Sleep Over Generation Z." *Forbes Magazine*, 11 Aug. 2017, www.forbes.com/ sites/ashleystahl/2017/08/11/why-democrats-should-be-losing-slee p-over-generation-z/#2964d53a7878.

95   Jenkins, Ryan. "4 Reasons Generation Z Will Be the Most Different Generation." *Inc.com*, Inc., 11 Jan. 2017, www.inc.com/ ryan-jenkins/who-is-generation-z-4-big-ways-they-will-be-different. html.

96   Smith, Tamsin. "Philanthro-Teens on the March." *The Huffington Post, TheHuffingtonPost.com*, 12 June 2011, www.huffingtonpost. com/tamsin-smith/philanthroteens-on-the-ma_b_847755.html.

97   Parker, Kim, et al. "Generation Z Looks a Lot Like Millennials on Key Social and Political Issues." *Pew Research Center's*

Social & Demographic Trends Project, Pew Research Center's Social & Demographic Trends Project, 18 Jan. 2019, www. pewsocialtrends.org/2019/01/17/generation-z-looks-a-lot-like-millennials-on-key-social-and-political-issues/.

98   Twenge, Jean M. "Have Smartphones Destroyed a Generation?" *The Atlantic*, Atlantic Media Company, 19 Mar. 2018, www.theatlantic.com/magazine/archive/2017/09/has-the-smartphone-destroyed-a-generation/534198/.

99   Newswire, MultiVu - PR. "New Cigna Study Reveals Loneliness at Epidemic Levels in America." *Multivu*, www.multivu.com/players/English/8294451-cigna-us-loneliness-survey/.

100   Bethune, Sophie. "Gen Z More Likely to Report Mental Health Concerns." *Monitor on Psychology*, American Psychological Association, Jan. 2019, www.apa.org/monitor/2019/01/gen-z.

101   Olshansky, S. Jay, et al. "A Potential Decline in Life Expectancy in the United States in the 21st Century." *New England Journal of Medicine*, vol. 352, no. 11, 2005, pp. 1138–1145., doi:10.1056/nejmsr043743.

102   "Video Games May Be a Part of the 2024 Olympics." *Fortune*, fortune.com/2017/08/09/video-games-2024-olympics/.

103   Twenge, Jean M. "Have Smartphones Destroyed a Generation?" *The Atlantic*, Atlantic Media Company, 19 Mar. 2018, www.theatlantic.com/magazine/archive/2017/09/has-the-smartphone-destroyed-a-generation/534198/.

104   Ibid.

105   "Loneliness and Social Isolation as Risk Factors for Mortality: A Meta-Analytic Review." *Perspectives on Psychological Science*, journals.sagepub.com/doi/abs/10.1177/1745691614568352.

106   "What We Do Together: The State of Associational Life in America." Prepared by the Vice Chairman's Staff of the Joint Economic Committee at the Request of Senator Mike Lee. https://

www.lee.senate.gov/public/_cache/files/b5f224ce-98f7-40f6-a814-8602696714d8/what-we-do-together.pdf.

107 "Is 'Gen Z' Equipped to Finance Retirement?" *Asppa.org*, 3 Nov. 2017, www.asppa.org/news-resources/browse-topics/'gen-z'-equipped-finance-retirement.

108 "Skipping School: Gen Z Entrepreneurs Make Their Own Way." *Online Schools Center*, www.onlineschoolscenter.com/skipping-school/.

109 Ibid.

110 "Beyond Millennials: The Next Generation of Learners." *Pearson*. Aug 2018. https://www.pearson.com/content/dam/one-dot-com/one-dot-com/global/Files/news/news-annoucements/2018/The-Next-Generation-of-Learners_final.pdf

111 Jeremy Finch, "What is Generation Z, and What Does It Want?" *Fast Company*, May 4, 2015, http://www.fastcompany.com/3045317/what-is-generation-z-and-what-does-it-want.

112 "Beyond Millennials: The Next Generation of Learners." *Pearson*. Aug 2018. https://www.pearson.com/content/dam/one-dot-com/one-dot-com/global/Files/news/news-annoucements/2018/The-Next-Generation-of-Learners_final.pdf

113 Fromm, Jeff, and Angie Read. *Marketing to Gen Z the Rules for Reaching This Vast and Very Different Generation of Influencers.* AMACOM, 2018.

114 "Skipping School: Gen Z Entrepreneurs Make Their Own Way." *Online Schools Center*, www.onlineschoolscenter.com/skipping-school/.

115 Ibid.

116 "Skipping School: Gen Z Entrepreneurs Make Their Own Way." *Online Schools Center*, www.onlineschoolscenter.com/skipping-school/.

117 Ibid.

118   "Beyond Millennials: The Next Generation of Learners." *Pearson.* Aug 2018. https://www.pearson.com/content/dam/one-dot-com/ one-dot-com/global/Files/news/news-annoucements/2018/ The-Next-Generation-of-Learners_final.pdf

119   Ibid.

120   "What We Do Together: The State of Associational Life in America." Prepared by the Vice Chairman's Staff of the Joint Economic Committee at the Request of Senator Mike Lee. https://www. lee.senate.gov/public/_cache/files/b5f224ce-98f7-40f6-a814-8602696714d8/what-we-do-together.pdf.

121   "Beyond Millennials: The Next Generation of Learners." *Pearson.* Aug 2018. https://www.pearson.com/content/dam/one-dot-com/ one-dot-com/global/Files/news/news-annoucements/2018/ The-Next-Generation-of-Learners_final.pdf

122   "Gen Z Is Shaping a New Era of Learning: Here's What You Should Know." *LinkedIn Learning*, learning.linkedin. com/blog/learning-thought-leadership/gen-z-is-shaping-a-ne w-era-of-learning--heres-what-you-should-kn.

123   "Generation Z Enters the Workforce." *Deloitte Insights*, www2.deloitte.com/insights/us/en/ focus/technology-and-the-future-of-work/ generation-z-enters-workforce.html#endnote-sup-14?trk=l ilblog_12-18-18_gen-z_tl&cid=70132000001AyziAAC.

124   "How to Effectively Communicate with Generation Z in the Workplace." *GetApp Lab*, 20 Nov. 2017, lab.getapp.com/ communicate-with-generation-z/.

125   "Skipping School: Gen Z Entrepreneurs Make Their Own Way." *Online Schools Center*, www.onlineschoolscenter.com/ skipping-school/.

126   "Gen Z Is Shaping a New Era of Learning: Here's What You Should Know." *LinkedIn Learning*, learning.linkedin.

com/blog/learning-thought-leadership/gen-z-is-shaping-a-ne
w-era-of-learning--heres-what-you-should-kn.

127   White, John. "Learn Why Top Gen Zers Are Skipping School to
Become Entrepreneurs." *Inc.com*, Inc., 11 Sept. 2017, www.inc.com/
john-white/learn-why-top-gen-zers-are-skipping-school-to-beco.
html.

128   Ibid.

129   "Prada's Revenues Buoyed by Refined Digital Strategy."
Heraldstandard.com, 15 Mar. 2019, www.heraldstandard.com/
world_news_ap/prada-s-revenues-buoyed-by-refined-digital-strategy/
article_c251f175-10db-58ee-a3c3-84d1c5a1c6d4.html.

130   "Influencer Marketing Statistics." *TapInfluence*, www.tapinfluence.
com/influencer-marketing-statistics/.

131   "Activating B2B Influencers across Earned, Owned, Shared
& Paid Media." *Marketing Land*, 16 July 2018, marketin-
gland.com/activating-b2b-influencers-across-earned-owne
d-shared-paid-media-243996.

132   "2018: The Year of Influencer Marketing for B2B
Brands." *Marketing Land*, 21 May 2018, marketin-
gland.com/2018-the-year-of-influencer-marketin
g-for-b2b-brands-240357.

133   "Gen Z Engaging with 10 Hours of Online Content a Day."
Marketing Tech News, www.marketingtechnews.net/news/2018/
feb/09/gen-z-engaging-10-hours-online-content-day/.

134   "How to Organize Your YouTube Channel." *iMatrix*, 4 Sept. 2018,
imatrix.com/blog/how-to-organize-your-youtube-channel/.

135   Dua, Tanya. "Four Things Brands Need to Know about
Gen Z." *Digiday*, 9 Apr. 2015, digiday.com/marketing/
four-things-brands-need-know-gen-z/.

136   Hodak, Brittany. "As Gen Z Reshapes the Social Media
Landscape, Marketers Need to Be Open to Change." *Adweek*,

Adweek, 29 Nov. 2018, www.adweek.com/brand-marketing/
as-gen-z-reshapes-the-social-media-landscape-marketers
-need-to-be-open-to-change/.

137   Minor, Dylan, and John Morgan. "CSR as Reputation Insurance."
University of California, Berkeley, faculty.haas.berkeley.edu/rjmorgan/
csr as reputation insurance.pdf.

138   "Generation Z: The Coming of (Shopping) Age." *ContentSquare,*
go.contentsquare.com/genz.

139   Salpini, Cara. "Gen Z Twice as Likely to Convert on Mobile." *Retail
Dive,* 25 July 2017, www.retaildive.com/news/gen-z-twice-as-likely-t
o-convert-on-mobile/447867/.

140   "Success Story: Adidas Used Snapchat to Drive an 18% Boost in
Store Visits." *Snap Business,* forbusiness.snapchat.com/inspiration/
adidas.

141   "When It Comes to Gen Z, Forget Everything You Know about
Brand Loyalty." *Vision Critical,* www.visioncritical.com/blog/
gen-z-brand-loyalty.

142   Ibid.

143   Fahey, Mark. "Everyone-and Your Mom-Is Using Emojis at
Work." *CNBC,* 8 Sept. 2015, www.cnbc.com/2015/09/08/
emojis-at-work-emails.html.

ABOUT THE AUTHOR

Sarah Weise is the founder and CEO of award-winning market research company Bixa (www.bixaresearch.com). Through qualitative and quantitative research, Sarah helps companies unravel the "why" behind customer behavior and make confident decisions about their brands and products, and envision radically intuitive experiences. Sarah lectures at Georgetown University's McDonough School of Business on marketing strategy for the next generation of customers. She is a co-founder of UX Masters Academy, and she speaks at conferences worldwide including MozCon, Digital Summit, Internet Summit, UXPA International, and Content Marketing Conference. Have you made it to the end of this bio? Really? Sign up for emails at www.instabrainbook.com and Sarah will send you a free 7-day "snackable" course on marketing to Generation Z with short emails, skimmable points, and possibly the key to world... er, brand domination.

Made in the USA
Monee, IL
23 March 2021